HEADLINES AND DEADLINES

Aileen O'Meara

Kathleen O'Meara

BLACKWATER PRESS

ISBN
0 86121641 5

Cover Photograph © Kate Horgan.

© Aileen O'Meara
Kathleen O'Meara

Produced in Ireland by
Blackwater Press
c/o Folens Publishers
8 Broomhill Business Park,
Tallaght, Dublin 24.

INTRODUCTION

The genesis of this book came from requests from students to talk about our jobs and how we ourselves got into journalism. Despite being affected by the media every day, there has been an information gap when it comes to practical information about the Irish media.

This book hopefully changes that situation.

Headlines and Deadlines is divided into three sections; The Press, Broadcasting, and Jobs and the Future.

The Press section deals with the daily, Sunday and evening newspapers, and brings the reader into the newsroom of the *Irish Times* and the *Sunday Tribune*, as well as interviews with key print journalists. We also look at the world of magazines, the provincial press and the specialist press.

In Broadcasting, there is a history of RTE, a look at RTE Radio and Television services, as well as the growing independent sector.

Jobs and the Future examines jobs in the media, and comprises interviews with working journalists, from the freelance to the public relations consultant. We look at the growing area of new technology which is going to change everything about future employment in the media.

We have provided a directory of relevant names and addresses in the media industry in Ireland in the final pages of the book.

As a practical insight into Irish journalism today, we hope this book goes some way to fill the information gap.

Aileen O'Meara
Kathleen O'Meara

ABOUT THE AUTHORS

Aileen O'Meara is a Producer and Reporter on the Pat Kenny Show on RTE's Radio One. A graduate of University College, Galway and Dublin City University (Diploma in Journalism) Aileen worked for a number of years in print journalism before coming to radio.

She was twice awarded A.T. Cross awards for her work on *The Sunday Tribune* and *The Irish Press*.

Kathleen O'Meara currently works as a Special Advisor to Minister of State Eithne Fitzgerald T.D. A graduate of University College, Galway, she holds a Diploma in Journalism from Dublin City University. She spent five years as a journalist in the RTE Newsroom, working on both television and radio as a reporter, sub-editor, and presenter. Kathleen has also worked as Press Officer for the Labour Party and as a Freelance Journalist.

To Mam and Dad

ACKNOWLEDGEMENTS

We would like to say a particular "thank you" to all those whom we interviewed for material for this book, for their time and cooperation. Journalists who are used to conducting the interview often find it hard to be on the other side of the questions, and we appreciate their interest. Without them *Headlines and Deadlines* would not have been possible.

A special word of thanks to the staff at the RTE Library, in particular Sé, for invaluable assistance, and Michael Flanagan in the *Sunday Tribune* library.

To Anna O'Donovan and Rachel O'Connor of Blackwater Press.

On a more personal level we would like to say "thank you" to Cathal and Kevin and Mark for their patience, support and encouragement during the early mornings, late nights and weekends the *Headlines and Deadlines* was written. And to all our friends whose constant "How is the book going?" spurred us on.

FOREWORD

Diversity of editorial control, the shadow of conglomerate ownership, and the rights of Irish people to have their news and public debates in a context which reinforces their sense of cultural identity are now all at the centre of our concerns about the future of the broadcasting and print media in Ireland.

We do not know, as this book goes to print, what the future of the Irish Press group will be, but the debate opened by the struggle for survival faced by this important player has at last forced us to ask questions about the role newspapers play in our cultural life, and recognise the need to take the necessary steps to ensure a healthy indigenous Irish media industry.

Broadcasting faces challenge and change. Local radio is now as rooted in the communities of Ireland as are regional and local newspapers. After only a short number of years local radio is making a significant contribution of the cultural life of the Ireland which lives outside Dublin. The growth of community radio is also going to be an important development in the next few years.

RTE as the national broadcaster too stands at a crossroads and I look forward to the response to the issues and questions posed in the Green Paper on Broadcasting, which will shape the changes in our legislative framework.

A publication such as *Headlines and Deadlines* comes at an opportune time. It charts a map through the media industry. Packed with information, it is an essential handbook for any student of the media. To any would-be journalist, and I know there are many, it will be required reading.

Headlines and Deadlines provides us with an extremely valuable resource. The authors have set out an overview of media structures and this will help in understanding the complexity of the challenge facing us.

Minister for Arts, Culture and the Gaeltacht
June 1995

CONTENTS

SECTION 1: THE PRESS

SECTION 2: BROADCASTING

SECTION 3: JOBS AND THE FUTURE

THE PRESS

Introduction

The Irish newspaper industry is at a crossroads.

A combination of factors - new technology, competition from Britain, high production and wage costs, high VAT rates and a trend towards falling readership means that over the coming decade, Irish national newspapers will have to make sweeping changes in order to adapt.

At a time when huge conglomerates are dominating the world media, the daily newspaper market in Ireland is dominated by one company: the Independent Group.

Owned by Tony O'Reilly, it commands ownership of not only the largest selling daily, the *Irish Independent*, but a range of Sunday, daily and provincial papers.

Like the *Independent, The Irish Times*, the *Press* and the *Cork Examiner* have a long history. The main dailies in Ireland all trace their origins back to the last century, and have seen off the huge changes in technology and communications that have come their way so far.

A shadow currently hangs over the Irish daily market - the future of the *Irish Press* group. Uncertainty hangs over its ownership - will a British concern come in, or a reputed Irish consortium take control?

And as Irish and foreign owned broadcasting stations bring their satellite-trained news to Irish television screens, will more and more Irish people take their news from broadcasting and ignore newspapers, and how will the newspaper industry adapt?

More English newspapers are gaining a foothold in Ireland, especially in the Sunday market. The recent decision of the *Sunday Times* to open a full time office in Dublin indicates their faith in building sales in Ireland, and their price drop is sending shudders through the market.

Newspapers in many ways lead public moods and reflect the culture of the community; opinion makers read newspapers to get their insights into the issues of the day; and the one striking trend in Irish newspapers that has received little attention so far is the lack in Ireland now of a so-called "right-wing" paper. With the huge social changes in Ireland, and the growing urbanisation of the population, all the papers reflect a liberal view on change - that greater individual freedom is correct, that there needs to be more separation of Church and State. There is no paper now that questions that trend, or reflects the views of people who oppose or question many of these changes.

Perhaps the next century will see the evolution of such a newspaper, and bring greater diversity to the Irish media market.

This chapter delves into the background of the main Irish newspapers, and also gives an insight into the production of a newspaper from team level to individual journalist.

It shows not only the complexity of newspaper production, but hopefully some of the excitement and variety involved in the daily work of bringing a newspaper to the reader every day.

1 INDEPENDENT AND IRISH

The National Daily Newspapers

At a time when fewer people are buying newspapers and relying on radio and television for their news, it seems there are more and more titles to choose from.

In Ireland, people not only have a choice of a range of Irish titles, they have the full range of English-based ones as well.

But it could be that the cut-throat competition may soon reduce the numbers. The *Irish Press* group, with 600 jobs, faces uncertainty due to continuing readership falls and financial insecurity. The *Independent* group, however, goes from strength to strength, dominating the daily newspaper market.

MORE THAN NEWS

Newspapers are not just about giving the news.

Today, newsrooms are swamped by the sheer availability of choice; every day, a news editor has to choose what to put in and what to leave out, what to highlight, what to reduce. A constant eye must be kept on what the electronic media is doing; nowadays big news gets around the world in seconds.

And because many newspapers can be rendered out of date by the time they appear in the shops the next morning, they have responded by publishing more background and analysis material, more actual information than a radio or screen can convey.

While the immediacy of a news story is often caught best by the electronic media, little can rival the newspaper's wide coverage of an important issue, and the personality and human touch it brings to the reader.

Although it is a "news" "paper", the reader is getting a product, or a package of things.

The news is usually on page one to three with the foreign news on succeeding pages.

Then there are features in the middle and sport towards the back.

And the death notices, the crossword, the letters page, the editorial, the fashion news, and what's on the television and radio for the coming day.

The newspaper that you buy - in its content and production - has become more sophisticated by technology, and that same technology has produced much more news to choose from.

THE IRISH PAPERS

Ireland has a varied and widely read press, from *The Irish Times* to the popular tabloid *Star*.

The daily newspaper market is dominated by the *Irish Independent*, its biggest seller, and the *Star* is closely followed by *The Irish Times* in readership.

Of the five national daily newspapers - the *Irish Independent*, *The Irish Times*, the *Star*, the *Irish Press* and the *Cork Examiner* – all except one are produced in Dublin, some within walking distance of each other.

TYPES OF PAPERS

The *Star* and the *Irish Press* are tabloid newspapers. They are small in size, easy to read, and have bigger headlines and photographs. Unlike England, the Irish newspaper market is not dominated by the tabloid style, which goes after personality rather than news, using populist angles and there is more emphasis on sport and television.

The others - such as the *Independent* and *The Irish Times* - are "broadsheet" or "quality" papers, more likely to be read by the professional classes. News, particularly political, business and foreign, gets far greater coverage in these papers.

Ireland's largest daily newspaper controls over 34% of the morning market, and it is part of the Independent Group of newspapers, owned by Tony O'Reilly. The Group also includes the *Star*, the *Evening Herald* and the *Sunday Independent*, and it owns a share in the *Sunday Tribune*, the *Sunday World* and a number of provincial papers.

The first issue of the *Irish Independent* appeared in 1891. William Martin Murphy founded it to quash the then monopoly of the *Freeman's Journal*.

When Tim Harrington became editor in 1904, he introduced what was then a major innovation - the use of plenty of photographs throughout the paper. The same year, it moved to Middle Abbey Street, and the "new look" Irish Independent was launched in January 1905. With sales of 25,000 a day in the beginning, it rose to 40,000 in three years – a huge success.

As the *Freeman's Journal* declined, the *Independent* prospered.

After the 1916 Rising, William Martin Murphy wrote an editorial denouncing the rebellion, reflecting what was then the popular mood.

When the *Freeman's Journal* closed in 1924, Murphy bought the titles.

During the 1920s, the paper was identified with the pro-Commonwealth position, and it supported Fine Gael during the 1930s.

In 1973, Tony O'Reilly, one of Ireland's richest men, took over the Independent group.

Now it is called Independent Newspapers Plc, and it is part of a worldwide publishing and communications company, with the O'Reilly operations stretching from Ireland to Australia, South Africa, France and Mexico, in regional newspapers, the electronic media, outdoor advertising and a private bus fleet in Melbourne, Australia.

Despite the international interests, Independent Newspapers remains a predominantly Irish company, with the majority of its turnover and profits coming from Irish operations.

Launched on the Irish market in February 1988, a joint venture between Independent Newspapers and the British Express group, the newest tabloid on the Irish market is now second only to the *Irish Independent* in daily sales.

"Research shows that news is not a big motivation for people who buy pop papers," said Gerry McGuinness, the joint chairman of the *Star*, when it was launched.

Most of the paper is now produced at its works in Terenure in south Dublin, but its 50-50 partnership with Express Newspapers remains the same. Perhaps this arrangement points to the future for more Irish newspapers facing growing competition from across the water.

After a bumpy start, and lower than expected sales, it has been steadily increasing over the years. When it began, half of its editorial copy came from its British edition; by 1993, over 95% of the content was originated and produced in Ireland, with continued reliance on the British edition for soccer coverage.

THE IRISH TIMES

PRICE 55p (incl. VAT) 55p meeting note   DUBLIN, MONDAY, FEBRUARY 13, 1995   No. 44,134   CITY

With its colour supplements, its full time correspondents in Africa, Moscow and Washington, and its strength in the broadsheet daily market, *The Irish Times* has come a long way since it was founded over 100 years go.

Major Lawrence Knox started the present-day *Irish Times* in 1859. He revived the original *Irish Times*, first published between 1823 and 1825, then based at Lower Abbey Street in Dublin.

In the beginning, it came out three times a week, and it cost a penny.

It went daily 14 weeks later.

Even then, it was considered a conservative newspaper, and the organ of the Protestant ascendancy for many years.

It gradually progressed under the stewardship of Major Knox, and by 1873, it was publishing 12 pages.

Knox died in 1873, and Sir John Arnott took over. A few years later, in 1882 it moved to its familiar premises in Westmoreland Street, where it remains to this day.

The busy subs' desk in The Irish Times.   Photograph: Kate Horgan.

By the 1890s, it was considered the most prosperous newspaper in Ireland, and Arnott was said to be earning £30,000 a year.

In the late Fifties and early Sixties, the paper's circulation was in decline. Its revival began from 1963 under the editorship of Douglas Gageby, a former *Irish Press* journalist, who introduced many innovations and new journalists. Investigative journalism and a radical new women's page became the hallmarks of a rejuvenated newspaper, with a strong "liberal" ethos, particularly on social matters.

From being the anti-establishment voice of a minority, it has now, with the changing social trends in Irish society, become the voice of the establishment.

It describes itself as having "a liberal ethos", and a few years ago, Conor Brady attributed the increasing sales to an increase in the levels of literacy, and to the growing urbanisation of Irish society. "In cultural terms, more people find it easier to identify with the liberal ethos of the newspaper."

The Irish Times is run by a trust. This was set up in 1974 by its owners to secure *The Irish Times* for the future and ensure its continued independence.

The Memorandum and Articles of Association of the company set out a number of principles and obligations, the first of which is to publish *The Irish Times* "as an independent newspaper free from any form of personal or of party political, commercial, religious or other sectional control".

The Trust is a company limited by guarantee without shareholders, and a charitable foundation was established which ultimately will benefit from the profits of that company.

There are seven governors of the Trust - appointed as being broadly representative of the community throughout the whole of Ireland – along with the editor, and six other directors.

Never in its 60 years has the *Irish Press* newspaper group been faced with such uncertainty.

With huge financial losses, unprecedented falls in circulation and a tough legal battle over shares ownership, the de Valera family faces difficult choices in the coming years.

The *Irish Press* was founded by Eamon de Valera at a time when the Irish newspaper market cried out for a voice that reflected the nationalist opinion and movement in the country; the Civil War was over, and the Cumann na nGaedhael government was in power.

On 5 September 1931, the sister of Patrick and Willie Pearse, and the patriots, started the presses for the final trial run of the *Irish Press* in Burgh Quay, and a new newspaper title was on its way.

Back in 1927, at the second Fianna Fail Ard Fheis, leader Eamon de Valera had announced the intention to launch a newspaper. £200,000 was needed in capital; shares were bought by ordinary people all over Ireland, and de Valera collected an estimated half a million dollars in the United States.

The Irish Press's first editorial said: "Our intention is to be the voice of the people, to speak for them, to give utterance to their ideals, to defend them against slander and false witness.

"Our ideal, culturally, is an Irish Ireland, an Ireland aware of its own greatness, sure of itself, conscious of the spiritual forces which have formed it into a distinct people having its own language and customs and a traditionally Christian philosophy of life. The realisation of those ideals calls for one quality more than any other - the honesty that is above question. We have given ourselves the motto: Truth in the News. We shall be faithful to it."

Controlled by the de Valera family, for many years the rivalry between the *Press* and the *Independent* continued; in the beginning, the *Press* was excluded from the newspaper train and lots of outlets by the other two titles.

But it was a huge success; it was instantly popular, mainly with a rural readership, and in 1949, the *Sunday Press* was launched, followed by the *Evening Press* in 1954.

Up to the late Sixties, the paper flourished, having gained a huge rural readership.

But since the Seventies, falling circulation and falling profits have beset the group. It is the daily that is now in the most trouble, financially and in terms of circulation.

In 1989, to help restore its financial base, the group invited American publisher Ralph Ingersoll to take a 50 % share in the company.

But the arrangement soon turned sour, and what should have been the beginning of a turn-around for the troubled *Irish Press* became a lengthy legal battle over control and funding. In the summer of 1994, the High Court ruled that Ingersoll should sell his stake in Irish Press Newspapers, back to its owners, *Irish Press* Plc., but further legal battles ensued.

A new investor is now required. Tony O'Reilly of Independent Newspapers bought a 24.9% interest, but the Competition Authority found this was an abuse of a dominant position, and against competition rules.

On target to lose £4m this year, a big investor is needed.

Ten years ago, the *Sunday Press*, *Irish Press* and *Evening Press* were selling over one and a half million copies every week; by June of 1994 that figure had fallen to just over 700,000.

The Cork Examiner

No. 53,729   FRIDAY MORNING, FEBRUARY 3, 1995   Price 80p (inc. VAT)

When the Cork Examiner management appointed 34-year-old Brian Looney as the new editor of their flagship the *Cork Examiner* last year (1994), they surprised some observers and insiders.

Because Looney, though from Cork, had worked for the rival Independent group for most of his journalistic career, and he was seen as an outsider.

But they needed to do something radical.

Losing circulation since 1981, it will be Mr Looney's job to turn the fortunes of "the Paper" around, and to institute a new strategy, including upgrading the paper's technology, and probably launching a Sunday

Examiner. The paper is expected to move to electronic page make-up in the near future.

Founded in 1841 by John Francis Maguire, the *Cork Examiner* has been in the control of the Crosbie family since 1872 when Mr Maguire died and Thomas Crosbie who had joined the paper at the age of 15, became the sole owner. Six years before the end of the century, the *Evening Echo* was founded.

Five generations of the Crosbie family have controlled Cork's own newspaper, and it is a Cork institution.

It is Ireland's only regional daily newspaper - that may be unique but it means it is neither a national daily nor a provincial paper, although it enjoys a huge dominance in its Munster base.

The company has invested heavily in new technology - it bought new presses in 1974 - and two of its titles have had direct input by journalists since 1986.

A DAY IN THE LIFE OF ...

THE IRISH TIMES NEWSROOM

FRIDAY 30 SEPTEMBER, PLANNING FOR EDITION OF SATURDAY 1 OCTOBER.

8.00am News editor Niall Kiely arrives in, having read the daily newspapers at home. Meets Renagh Holohan, assistant news editor, who is putting together the "Morning News schedule".

9.00am All is quiet. Renagh has listened to Morning Ireland, read the other papers, checked the diary.

The first of the reporters, Catherine Cleary is sent to cover an EAT (Employment Appeals Tribunal) involving a member of PDFORRA, the Defence Forces representative body.

Niall and Renagh sit at the newsdesk, a central area where the news editors, senior sub editors and chief sub editors sit, near where reporters, the photo desk and the subs desk can reach them.

The television, radios, fax machines and several telephones are within reach.

To the right of the Desk the reporters sit at desks, piled high with notebooks, reports, books and papers. Each has a telephone and a computer.

The ATEX Irish Times system is networked, a new technology system in which all "copy" is typed in, assigned to queues and subbed and laid out by sub editors.

To the left of the newsdesk is the foreign news section, where the foreign editor and the sub editors sit.

To the far left sit the business section, with editorial staff, reporters and subs.

Behind the newsdesk is the photographic section where the photo editor sits, and photographers gather. There is also there the computerised library, the PA library on disk and sent down the ISDN line.

Everyone works with a computer in front of them.

10.00am Three reporters have been assigned; Michael Foley, part-time media correspondent, is writing the review of the week for page 2.

Peter Thompson, freelance, will go to the launch of the Lotto Millenium clock award to write a "colour" piece.

Political correspondent Geraldine Kennedy rings about the political feature for Saturday; the political staff spend most time in their office in Leinster House and do not come to *The Irish Times* newsroom. In Leinster House they have a networked computer, a fax and telephone.

Taoiseach Albert Reynolds is meeting Boris Yeltsin in Shannon, but it's decided that the political staff in Dublin won't go; local reporter Arthur Quinlan will cover it.

11.00am Renagh and Niall listen to the 11 O'Clock news headlines on RTE radio before going upstairs to the news conference in the editor's office area.

11.30am At the first news conference of the day Renagh Holohan circulates the morning news schedule, with the main stories of the day, plus the news features listed.

There's a post mortem. Niall Kiely explains that they didn't have the reporters available to make a bigger story of the Kerry Barrett case (father not allowed bury his daughter in his mausoleum). The *Irish Independent* had a big spread on the same story, with photographs of the dead girl and the family.

Decisions are made at the meeting - attended by section heads from business, features, photos, and sport, to assign stories to inside news features pages.

Decisions are made about some of the day's stories being covered - the Reynolds/ Yeltsin meeting, ESB meeting, mostly events happening that day - Ministers speaking, EAT, launch of booklet, Gerry Adams in USA.

Patsy Murphy, the Features Editor, outlines the contents of the Weekend Supplement. These features have already gone to production due to the earlier deadlines.

The meeting finishes after half an hour, some of the stories being discussed, pictures needed, and it's back to business.

Reporters, who work a nine-day fortnight in *The Irish Times*, are arriving as the morning goes on.

The Irish Times has a lot of specialist reporters. There are 34 newsroom staff including the desk.

Renagh Holohan starts assigning stories to staff on duty, some follow ups, some from the diary of events of the day.

All the time, her telephones are ringing, the fax machine is spewing out press releases and statements, and the radio news is being monitored.

Page two must go early, and Michael Foley is put under pressure to finish the review. The profile of the man believed to have begun the plague in India, has come from the Foreign Section.

"If it's away at 12, I'm happy," says Niall Kiely.

"If we miss the early edition, we miss the home deliveries, that's 3 to 4,000 copies a day now."

The Catholic Press office rings with details of the profile of the new Bishop of Killaloe; Religious Affairs Correspondent will do a piece before he plans his feature on next week's Synod.

Putting the finishing touches to The Irish Times.   Photograph: Kate Horgan.

12.30pm Arthur Quinlan rings from Shannon. "Yeltsin won't get off the plane!" exclaims Renagh to Niall Kiely, and suddenly an ordinary story becomes big news. The photo desk decides on photographs, colour will be needed for the front page. Cartoonist Martyn Turner may be notified.

News editor Niall Kiely consults the "flat sheets" - the layout of the pages on small grids that will be used to design and assign stories for the rest of the day.

1.00pm The lunchtime news is monitored, including the Yeltsin story which is now the main headline. Further reporters are assigned; Seamus Martin in Moscow is tracked down, so is Conor O'Clery in Washington on previous similar incidents from the Yeltsin USA tour; Geraldine Kennedy will watch it from Leinster House for political reaction there.

3.00pm Second news conference held, this time more detailed newslist. News and photos are coordinated and planned.

A further story on the Indian plague with an Irish angle is discussed.

The newsroom fills up. A mandatory NUJ meeting is called, over the issue of responsibility for the new "News Digest" column on the front page. This takes an hour and holds up stories.

At the desk, Dick Ahlstrom arrives in to take over from Renagh Holohan.

5.00pm Short news conference.

Copy is coming in, is subbed and read again, and assigned to pages.

Chief sub designs pages according to information supplied from the newsdesk, and computerised layout is planned. Subs will write captions, headlines and design space according to information given.

6.00pm Television news monitored.

Martyn Turner cartoon arrives by fax, greeted by smiles. It shows a caricature of a surprised Taoiseach, watching a glass bottle containing a message, as it bounces onto the red carpet at the end of the airplane's steps. Beside him, the Taoiseach's adviser says "At last.. a message from President Yeltsin." The cartoon says everything the reporters cannot say.

Paul Murray sends the computerised update on the Yeltsin arrival in Moscow to Geraldine Kennedy; he's given the reasons for his non-appearance.

The front page is discussed. The Kerry Barrett story will make page one, to include the High Court battle over the burial, and the comments of the family in Kerry.

7.00pm The four telephones on Dick Ahlstrom's desk continue to ring; press releases and statements continue to spew from the fax machine.

He sends the Arthur Quinlan story on Yeltsin from Shannon, plus Seamus Martin's Moscow update, to Geraldine Kennedy, where she will pull the elements together.

Reporter John Maher prepares the front-page News Digest, the double column of summaries of the paper's main stories.

7.15pm The editorial heads decide to lead with Cliff Taylor's exclusive story on the ESB's cost-cutting plans.

Stories for the inside pages are being assigned and checked before being sent to the caseroom. Reporter Christine Newman speaks to the Barrett family, and tells Ahlstrom they've decided to go ahead with the burial despite the injunction. He contacts a local reporter, and arranges a photographer to be at the Saturday funeral.

8.00pm Garth Wilton maps page five, and assigns the background and court report on the Barrett story. Further stories are placed.

10.00pm Correspondent Jackie Gallagher finalises the TEAM story; local reporter Gerard Colleran has got more details on the Barrett story for page one.

10.30pm New copy changes the Barrett story. The family have now decided not to go ahead with the burial after all; Dick Ahlstrom takes the fresh copy from Gerard Colleran over the phone and writes it into the system himself.

12.30pm Downstairs in the caseroom, the printing machines are being prepared, and all but the front page is ready to go. There's a colour photograph of Jackie Kennedy missing; when it can't be found on time, a black and white one is used instead.

The first edition begins printing soon afterwards; within a few hours, it will be on the streets and transported around the country.

TIM HASTINGS, REPORTER

Delivering The News

Tim Hastings, Industrial Correspondent with the *Irish Independent*, finds his stories all over the place.

"In pubs, over cups of coffee, often the last sentence in an interview situation," he said, responding to a query about the origins of his stories.

The man who brings us the stories of disputes, Labour Court hearings, rationalisations of semi-state companies, and sexual harassment cases in the Employment Appeals Tribunals, came into journalism through an unusual route.

"I had a BA in Economics and Politics from UCD and was a Dubliner," he said. "In 1977 there was a bias against both graduates and Dubliners in the provincial papers!"

"I got a job from John Healy in the *Western People* because I was prepared not only to write the stories, but to deliver the newspapers as well! I delivered 3,000 *Western People* every Tuesday."

A year in the *People* gave him a great training, he believes - not only in delivery techniques.

He learnt how to "write a story about everything". He did sport, court reporting, human interest stories, everything, and it gave him a grounding for the general reporting he did in the *Irish Press* for the next nine years.

Having done some industrial relations stories in the *Press* when the regular correspondent was away, he had a taste for that area when he moved as reporter to the *Irish Independent* in 1987. After a stint as a general reporter, he got his current specialist post.

"My job is very flexible. It means that when a big story is breaking, I stay with it right through, even if that means spending about three days stuck down in the Labour Court," he said.

Last summer (1994) was spent on the TEAM Aer Lingus dispute, providing daily copy "even when there wasn't anything happening."

He works an average eight-hour shift, starting around 11am and staying longer if the story demands it. "You write a 'holding' story for the country edition if it needs changing for the later city editions. Mostly the news editor will ask for a line on a story, and sometimes I'll have to do a News Analysis feature piece for inside as well."

The *Independent* has two news conferences, at 2.30 and 4.30 in the afternoon, and the correspondents will generally offer a story for the early ones and an update for later. His first story for the country edition is needed by about five in the evening. Generally, he finishes at about 8 or 9 at night.

Industrial Relations, with its coverage of sometimes complex disputes, requires considerable attention to detail, as well as knowledge of the business, political and economic areas.

Tim Hastings at his desk in the Irish Independent newsroom.   Photograph: Kate Horgan.

His sources? "Management and unions, and also some outsiders," he said.

"You come in, you make phone calls to your sources, you trawl, look at what the other papers are doing, follow up some leads, some hunches."

He spends an increasing amount of time on the telephone, but feels that it's also very important to meet people, and hence he'll meet them on the street, for lunch or a pint.

"The thing that's different about my brief is that a lot of the people I need to talk to are out all day - so I phone a lot of them at home. As well, I rely a lot on off-the-record briefings; you'll notice about the stories that Industrial Relations journalists do often have nobody at all quoted in them! By and large, the people I talk to don't want to be interviewed at all, unlike other areas where the press releases are flying at you from all angles."

Earlier, he had leaked a report on the number of expected job cuts in the ESB. How are reports leaked? "Basically by tracking people down. Sometimes you're working on an informed hunch that just needs to be confirmed, you get a bit from one quarter and back it up from another."

Building up trust with contacts takes time and patience, and if it works leads to the exclusive stories that are generated in the main by specialist correspondents with detailed knowledge of their areas.

And things are changing in the areas of Industrial Relations. "The standard old disputes of workers going out on strike are becoming a thing of the past," Tim said. "Now a lot more industrial relations are about equality disputes, training, privatisation of semi-states, it's a whole new agenda."

2 DIFFERENT DEADLINES

The Sunday and Evening Papers

THE SUNDAY PAPERS

Rarely has there been a more competitive era for Irish Sunday newspapers.

The British papers, in particular the Rupert Murdoch-owned *Sunday Times*, are proving a major challenge for the Irish quality Sunday newspapers, and there is intense competition amongst the Irish-owned Sundays.

Tony O'Reilly's Independent Newspapers dominates the Sunday market, fully owning or having a minority stake in all but one Irish-owned Sunday.

Independent Newspapers owns and controls the top two selling Sunday papers - the *Sunday World* and the *Sunday Independent*.

It holds a minority shareholding in the *Sunday Tribune*, and the *Sunday Press*.

The small *Sunday Business Post* is partly owned by a German investor along with Irish shareholders.

Small companies, like the *Sunday Tribune*, are suffering continued losses with falling circulation to the huge conglomerate that owns the *Sunday Times*.

In 1993, the *Sunday Times* opened a full-time office in Dublin, with several staff and a commitment to greater coverage of Irish stories, and this is now beginning to pay off, particularly with a fall in price.

The Irish Sunday market, however, is still dominated by its own: the *Sunday Independent* and the *Sunday World*, a broadsheet and tabloid newspaper both owned by Independent Newspapers.

The *Sunday Independent* has won the lead in the Republic, with its combination of opinionated columnists, detailed sports coverage and quality colour, while the *Sunday Press* has fallen into third place after its huge circulation in the 60s and 70s.

The Irish newcomer, the *Sunday Business Post*, remains an important paper amongst a market share, while the English *Sunday Mirror* and *Sunday People* claim a circulation close the the *Sunday Times*.

The *Sunday Business Post* has taken a share of the *Sunday Tribune's* market. At the same time, daily papers, especially the *Irish Times* and *The Irish Independent*, are bringing out special weekend supplements to fight the Sundays' circulation.

In 1973, magazine publishers Hugh McLaughlin and Gerry McGuinness founded the *Sunday World*, Ireland's first tabloid Sunday newspaper, and it quickly became a successful publishing venture;

within two years of its foundation, it had become profitable, and by the second half of 1976, its circulation passed that of the *Sunday Independent's*.

When the company that published it - the Creation Group - went into liquidation in 1975, the *Sunday World* was printed from its own premises at Terenure in Dublin, and as its main competitors experienced a fall in circulation, the *World* went up and up.

In early 1978, Tony O'Reilly's Independent Newspapers bought a controlling interest in Sunday Newspapers, the company that published the *Sunday World*, for £1.1m. Hugh McLaughlin agreed to sell his 54% shareholding in return for cash and Independent shares. Gerry McGuinness remained as Managing Director and retained his 42% shareholding.

By buying a majority stake in its competitor, Independent Newspapers sealed off a threat to its own *Sunday Independent*, while retaining the *World* as a separate entity.

In 1982, Independent Newspapers bought out Gerry McGuinness's 42% share, as part of the earlier agreement, and the *Sunday World* was valued at £6.3m. It generated pre-tax profits of £1m. - nearly half of the *Independent*'s overall profits.

The *Sunday World* remains Ireland's leading Sunday tabloid newspaper.

Its circulation last year was 207,615 in the Republic last year, with a further 68,777 in the North of Ireland, where it has always retained a significant readership.

It has retained its share over the ten years of its history, despite intense competition from the English

tabloids, the *Sunday People* and the *Sunday Mirror*, with a much lower cover price.

Sunday Independent

Founded in 1906 by William Martin Murphy, the man who created the *Irish Independent* a decade earlier, the *Sunday Independent* now has a commanding lead in the Sunday newspaper market.

With sales of almost 252,000 copies, the *Sunday Independent* remains the leading newspaper, having passed out competitors like the *Sunday Press*, in recent years. It has a market share of 23% of the Sundays, competing successfully with the growing number of British qualities in the Irish market.

With a high number of readers in the ABC 1 bracket, its combination of analysis, comment, politics and gossip has been a successful recipe. More than any other Sunday, the *Independent*'s wide range of opinion on politics, sport, media personalities and gossip with high quality colour and lifestyles coverage, has made it Ireland's most widely read Sunday newspaper. *(See Irish Independent in Chapter 1.)*

The Sunday Press

Founded in 1949 after the huge success of the *Irish Press*, the Sunday paper soon reached a substantial rural audience. Up the Sixties, with its mixture of personality stories, sports coverage and politics, it retained the top share of the Sunday market.

However, like its sister paper the *Irish Press*, it has declined in readership to the *Independent* since the 70s. New investment and editorial content is now urgently required to stop the continuing fall in circulation; last year's purchase of a shareholding in the Press group by Tony O'Reilly's Independent Newspapers is unlikely to make a significant difference to its fortunes.

It is widely felt that Independent Newspapers moved in to ensure that British publisher Conrad Black, who owns the Mirror group, could not buy a share in his biggest competitor in the Irish market. *(See Irish Press in Chapter 1.)*

THE SUNDAY
TRIBUNE

12 FEBRUARY 1995 VOL 16 NO 7   IRELAND'S QUALITY SUNDAY NEWSPAPER   • • • •PRICE: £1 (incl VAT), 90p sterling

Launched in November 1980 by businessman Hugh McLaughlin, the paper ceased publication two years later when the founder's company went into liquidation.

The title was then bought by Dr Tony Ryan, the millionaire chairman of Guinness Peat Aviation, and Vincent Browne, then editor of *Magill* magazine. It was relaunched in April 1983, and Mr Browne remained editor until his removal in January 1993 by the board of the newspaper.

Under Browne's editorship, the newspaper gained a reputation for independent journalism, hard-hitting political coverage, and award-winning investigative journalism.

In the 70s the paper went through a series of refinancing measures to offset huge losses and debts, including quotation on the Stock Exchange. When it appeared to have turned the corner in 1990, Mr Browne launched a Dublin freesheet, the *Dublin Tribune*, which was a financial failure, generating losses of over £1m.

Independent Newspapers bought a 29.99% share in the *Tribune* in November 1990, and the then Minister Desmond O'Malley prevented any increased shareholding under monopolies legislation.

As losses mounted to £2.34 million in 1991, two Independent directors were invited onto the Tribune board, and a financial executive was put in place.

When the *Dublin Tribune* closed down, losses increased and circulation fell. Further share issues and loans have been drawn down, and fresh capital is needed.

Former *Irish Times* and *Guardian* journalist, Peter Murtagh, replaced Vincent Browne as editor early in 1994, a few months after Mr Browne was removed by the Board. It is up to him to stem the losses, and offset the competition from the native *Sunday Business Post*, as well as the strengthening *Sunday Times*.

From a high of over 100,000, circulation in 1993 figures stood at 87,806.

THE SUNDAY BUSINESS POST

IRELAND'S FINANCIAL, POLITICAL, AND ECONOMIC NEWSPAPER

VOL 7, NO. 19   May 14 1995   PRICE £1

The newcomer on the crowded Sunday market, the *Sunday Business Post* was founded by four business journalists in 1989 with funding from the French based media company, Eurexpansion.

Aimed primarily at the business market, and ABC1 readership, the paper is a competitor in particular with the *Sunday Tribune*. Aimed at a target business readership, the circulation (1993) stands at under 30,000, and is considered to have achieved a stable readership and financial base.

Last year, the paper underwent a radical financial restructuring with the original French investor selling most of its shares, and the new investor is believed to be a German magazine publisher, Norman Rentrop Verlag, based in Bonn, with a 40% shareholding.

Eurexpansion retained a 10% holding, with 50% of the shareholding retained by the management group in Ireland, made up of chief executive Barbara Nugent, editor Damien Kiberd, and deputy editor Aileen O'Toole. Post Publications Ltd., which publishes the *Post,* reported a pre-tax profit for the first time in 1993, of £210,000.

ENGLISH SUNDAY NEWSPAPERS IN IRELAND

British Sunday newspapers sell over 100,000 copies in the north and south of Ireland every Sunday.

But in recent years, the competition of British-based newspapers in Ireland has become keener, both between each other and with the Irish Sundays themselves.

The main development in this area has been the decision of the *Sunday Times* to open an Irish office in Dublin, and staff a separate Irish edition of its paper.

PLUS: IRELAND'S TOP 7-DAY TV AND RADIO GUIDE

THE SUNDAY TIMES

No 8,909   28 MAY 1995   Price £1(IR or £1 (IRE) incl Vax

Sold in Ireland for several decades now, *The Sunday Times* launched a separate Irish edition in March 1993, and opened an Irish office with an Irish editor and Irish staff in 1994.

Owned in Britain by Rupert Murdoch's News International plc, a world-wide media corporation, the paper has strong resources and a huge British readership behind it.

However, in October 1995, its serialisation of the Jonathan Dimbleby book about Prince Charles brought its sales to over 100,000 - the same week, it reduced its cover price to 50p.

As a quality Irish Sunday, with a range of sections and a quality colour magazine, the new edition put Irish columnists and Irish stories onto a basically British newspaper.

While it has eaten into the sales of the *Sunday Tribune*, *Sunday Times* editor Alan Ruddock says their main competitors in the Irish market are the other British Sundays – the *Observer, Telegraph* and *Mail on Sunday* – between them selling over 60,000 papers in Ireland every Sunday.

THE SUNDAY MIRROR AND THE SUNDAY PEOPLE

Both large sellers in the tabloid market in Ireland on Sundays, the *Sunday Mirror* and the *Sunday People* are part of the British Mirror Group of Newspaper.

EVENING PAPERS

Evening papers have always held a special place in Irish journalism.

From a business point of view, the most competitive evening market remains the Dublin one, primarily aimed at a lucrative advertising market, and a large classifieds section aimed at Dublin readers.

Like the daily market, the Independent group maintains a lead with its tabloid sized popular *Evening Herald*, followed by the *Evening Press*.

But the competitive market is facing changes: fewer people are now buying papers in the evening.

In recent years, both of the Dublin evening papers have dropped sales, but the Press has suffered more - in 1991 for example, the *Herald* fell by 3.3% in sales,

while the *Evening Press* fell by 13.6%.

While the two Dublin based papers dominate the market, outside Dublin, there is the *Belfast Telegraph* in the North of Ireland, and the *Evening Echo*, published by the *Cork Examiner* in the Munster region.

Part of the Independent Newspapers stable, the *Evening Herald* started out as a broadsheet newspaper, founded shortly after the Irish Independent in 1891.

Now the largest-selling evening newspaper in the Republic, it sells over 90,000 copies in the Republic.

In recent years, the *Herald* has been published as a tabloid, revamped to give it a more urban and modern look.

Selling particularly strongly in the capital, the evening paper's formula of "What's On," sport and classifieds has made it a winner in Dublin.

Despite the overall drop in sales in the evening market, the *Herald* has retained over 50% of the national market, and its penetration of the Dublin market continues to increase.

For a long time the predominant evening newspaper, the *Evening Press* has remained one of the stronger titles in the faltering Press group of newspapers.

Founded in September 1954 by the de Valera family as part of the then vibrant and expanding newspaper market, the *Evening Press* has a strong classifieds section, good sports coverage, and retains its broadsheet form.

As a broadsheet, it was aimed then at the urban readership, and was founded at a time when its sister papers the *Irish Press* and the *Sunday Press* were thriving.

Its first editor was Douglas Gageby, who later became editor of *The Irish Times*.

Its circulation is under 60,000, a considerable distance behind the *Evening Herald*, a paper it outsold in past decades.

Affected by the overall fall in fortunes of the Press group, the *Evening Press* needs further investment to modernise and strengthen its appeal to increase circulation and battle against the stronger competitor.

Part of the Cork Examiner group, the *Cork Evening Echo* is the only evening paper serving the Munster region, and sells mainly in Cork city.

It dominates the city evening market.

Best for local city news, the Echo is a Cork institution and was founded over 100 years ago in 1882, 50 years after its sister paper, the *Cork Examiner*.

Belfast Telegraph

The North's leading evening daily newspaper is the *Belfast Telegraph*, founded in 1871 by two brothers, W and G Baird, who ran a printing company in the city.

It remained in the hands of the Baird family until 1961, when it was taken over by the Canadian media tycoon, Lord Roy Thomson, of the Thomson media empire.

This takeover was the first breach in the local ownership of Belfast newspapers, and it was a shock to the media confraternity in the city.

The Telegraph has a wide circulation across the North, with correspondents based across the province.

In recent years, in common with the other Belfast dailies, the *Belfast Telegraph* invested over £20m in new printing technology.

Its circulation according to UK figures is over 135,000.

The paper plans to move over to new production techniques which will make it among the most modern in Europe, with full colour facilities for use in some parts of the paper - it first went colour in 1985.

A WEEKEND IN...

THE SUNDAY TRIBUNE

FRIDAY, 23 SEPTEMBER 1994

5.00pm Things are getting hectic in the Business and Production departments, and the news features are being finalised. With the paper printed outside the buildings, its sections go in stages to the printers - the features magazine first; the business and some inside sports pages next, and news and final sports on Saturday evening.

By this time Friday, things are getting busy, and much of the paper is being finalised.

In Business, reporter Ursula Halligan is writing up an article on Bord Failte, having been talking to Minister Charlie McGreevy about his plans for the future of the organisation.

In news, features are being finalised; much of the larger articles are already done. In the Magazine section, they're already planning next week's cover, with the week's magazine already gone to the printers. In their office Features Editor Roslyn Dee and Design Consultant Gerry Sandford have spent the day mapping out the regular features for Sunday week's magazine.

Over in the subs area, production editor Paul Hopkins has "mapped" the pages of the business section, and his sub editors are placing copy. The pages are proofed by their editors before going to the printers that night.

The normal week for the Sunday Tribune staff begins on Tuesday, with the weekly editorial meeting on Tuesday morning. All editorial and production staff attend, where the paper is analysed, and stories for the coming week are discussed. A smaller meeting of the section editors is held after this; stories are chosen, reporters assigned.

On Wednesday, the colour pages of the features section are sent to the printers - transparencies (or trannies) for the fashion features are sent, and advertising copy also.

On Thursday, most of the features pages are sent, finished by 6.30 pm.

6.00pm In the subs area, production editor Paul Hopkins begins drawing up pages for Saturday's news section - the opinion and editorial pages in the centre.

In the nearby Sports department, four journalists are already working on pages to be finished that night.

Barrister Paul Burns reads all the copy given to him by the editor, he will work throughout Friday evening and all day Saturday. Copy that is potentially libellous or controversial must be read by Paul; he may suggest changes in the wording, or taking out information or moving it around.

Paul Hopkins in The Sunday Tribune Newsroom.

A story by reporter Diarmuid Doyle on a medical negligence action is carefully combed through, and changes are suggested; so also is an article by reporter Susan McKay on sexual harassment in the workplace.

Paul Hopkins' desk is the centre of the production area, where news editor Rory Godson liaises with him, where editor Peter Murtagh checks progress, and where the production department can see what's coming.

6.30pm Over at the Sports Department, editor Ger Siggins is planning his seven pages; the features sections - interviews, profiles, columns - have been designed and subbed by Friday night; four or five pages, depending on the amount of live coverage on the Saturday.

The colour photograph for the back page is an important consideration for Saturday - This week it will be a shot of a rugby match from Limerick. The game starts at 2.30; the photo will be ready and waiting by six, sent up by wire machine from the local hotel to the office in Dublin, where it is printed and brought around to the Tribune offices in time.

7.00pm Deputy business editor David Nally is finalising the business pages. There's a major feature on the tobacco industry being finalised, featured as a result of a big report on the effects of health warnings on the tobacco sales.

The markets page - stocks and unit trust prices - has been compiled; this is the most-read page after the front page of the Business section.

By Friday lunchtime, Goodman's deal with the banks, and Smurfit's rights issue had emerged as news stories; features, comment and regulars had been finished by Thursday evening.

....

SATURDAY, 24 SEPTEMBER 1994

10.30am It's quiet in the newsroom as reporters finalise late features and write news copy. Material is being taken over the phone from journalist Michael Hand in Cork, and typed into the news system; news editor Rory Godson will it read and make some small changes.

In the photo library, Bea McMunn is watching her computerised photograph machine, a dataphoto receiver, which can provide black and white, and colour photographs from the PA agency straight to her desk, from a central computer in London, via telephone wire.

A news conference is held in editor Peter Murtagh's office - attended by the editorial heads.

Rory Godson consults his A4 sized grid of the 24 pages of the paper's main section, with the ads

Features Editor, Roslyn Dee and Design Consultant, Gerry Sandford finalise the magazine cover in
The Sunday Tribune.   Photograph: Kate Horgan.

allocated, and the main features, the foreign, sport, editorial and letters assigned.

The foreign pages are finalised and are being subbed; copy mostly comes from regular correspondents and agency copy.

11.30am A meeting between the news editor and the editor decides that because of the high domestic news content, one page of foreign news will be dropped (down to 2), to increase the domestic news. The pages are remapped by Paul Hopkins to place Susan McKay's article on sexual harassment.

At noon, a meeting with Paul Hopkins assigns the stories on pages 6 and 7 and the pages are mapped accordingly.

The lead story - the role of Charles Haughey in the peace process is chosen; an exclusive by Northern Editor Ed Moloney, leading into a feature story inside.

Reporter Fergal Keane continues to update a feature on the TEAM Aer Lingus crisis.

Photographers have been assigned to today's events around the city, both news and features - there are four spaces kept for pictures from Saturday's stories.

Paul looks to Bea McMunn for a selection of colour photographs of Charles Haughey for the inside feature article.

In the production area, the finished page has come through a typesetter, it is put through bromide, onto bromide paper and is then developed through a processor, shot onto film.

Brian Goodwin "creates" the page on computer, based on Paul Hopkins' map. He maps the spaces for headlines, stories, photographs, bylines and ads. This map is then used by the subs to fill the spaces with copy and graphics.

He "reserves" the spaces for the photos, headings, breaking them all into column-based blocks on a grid on the screen. Each component gets a name to be placed in the queue.

12.15pm Colin Kerr, a freelance reporter, and photographer Anne Egan go to the airport to cover the TEAM meeting, and the arrival of reporter Susan O'Keeffe from England, back to face contempt charges over her refusal to reveal her sources to the Beef Tribunal.

Colin will work closely with Fergal Keane who is writing a feature on the TEAM crisis.

They must be back by 4pm with both copy and photos.

12.20pm Sub editor Evelyn Bracken subs back the Ed Moloney inside feature to make it fit. It's 166 lines over.

Photographer Derek Spiers returns with shots of Lord Mayor John Gormley, and leaves shortly afterwards for the Third World debt parade, starting at one o'clock.

1.00pm More sub editors arrive in the news and sports areas.

In the library, Michael Flanagan is available to provide sources of information at short notice to reporters.

He has 60,000 newspaper cuttings on 6 optical disks, based on information gathered since October 1990 when he began the computerised system. He also has access to "FT Profile" a computerised database, which contains all the British daily quality papers, and also *The Irish Times*. He also has magazines, reference material, the *Sunday Tribune* going back to its original days, and he has access to the Internet.

He keeps copies of the Irish daily newspapers and has the Irish Business Index, Keesings reference guides, and paper indexes of the Economist going back 5 years.

3.00pm Paul Hopkins chooses the photographs for Ed Moloney's feature on the peace process for pages 14 - 15. Derek Spiers, back from the march, suggests to Rory Godson and Paul the kind of photos he has. Rory has left his office to sit opposite Paul Hopkins to help map the news pages. They discuss lengths of stories in terms of column inches.

A part-time copy taker comes to take sports copy from the stringers around the country, over the telephone; some 15 stringers send in copy from far flung matches and sports events.

An early proof of page one is analysed; the foreign pages have gone to bromide; sub editor Maxine Jones works on the front page. Now everyone is working against the clock.

3.40pm Paul Hopkins designs page two. Derek Spiers looks at the contact sheets and offers a photograph from the Third World debt march. It will be placed on page one.

Sports pages are finalised; 15 minutes after a game is finished, the PA agency can give an up-to-date match report on the line.

3.50pm Reporter Michael Hand phones in copy, a colour piece on the Galway Oyster Festival.

5.15pm On the stone, where the finishing touches are put to the pages before they leave for the printers, Brian Goodwin puts the rules (thin black lines) on the news features pages. The subs work to finish page three. Diarmuid Doyle arrives in for the night reporter shift.

Page three is delayed - a story won't fit. Paul Hopkins shouts at barrister Paul Burns to read the headline in the medical negligence case before it goes.

6.25pm Page three is finished.

6.40pm The final touches to the sports pages are being made on the stone. The staff go for a pint. The first edition will hit the streets after eight o'clock.

KATIE HANNON, FREELANCE FEATURES WRITER

You Never Know what the Next Day will Bring

Life may be varied but you have very little time to yourself when you are a freelance journalist in Dublin.

Katie Hannon writes features, opinion and colour articles for the leading evening paper, the *Evening Herald*.

Being freelance, she's available at short notice for a variety of assignments for the paper, and works at all hours. "You can stay there all night if you want to," she says of writing up features for the following day.

Features take up the inside bulk of the tabloid paper, wrapped around the listings and *What's On* and the television in the middle, and the news and sports on the outer.

A graduate of the Rathmines College of Commerce Journalism course, and several years working on the RTE Aertel service, she joined the paper two years ago, writing feature articles and the Diary column. Since a staff writer went on leave a few months before, she's been writing an opinion column every Friday, and features and profiles on other days.

Unlike journalists who write for morning papers, most of Katie's deadlines are the day before printing.

News analysis articles are generally written by the afternoon before, though some on the morning itself. The *Herald* has four editions from mid-morning to early afternoon, and when she is assigned to a morning event, she has to write for several editions of the *Herald*, from ten o'clock for the first edition, right up to 1.30 for the final "four star" edition.

Outside the daily routine, she does interviews, like a recent "conveyor belt" interview with the skating stars Torvill and Dean, in Dublin, to promote their tour. She lined up behind a queue of journalists all getting an alloted 30 minutes with the stars in a Dublin hotel on a Sunday afternoon. Her feature interview was published as a two page spread a few days later.

She writes colour - such as the descriptive, often humorous piece on the appearance of Dick Spring at the Dail committee investigating the events leading up to the fall of the Fianna Fail-Labour partnership government. For that article, she filed copy at 1.30pm for an edition that hit the streets at 4pm that afternoon.

She writes features. She'd recently completed a two page spread with photos, two pages of an article on New Age Travellers in Dunmanway. A photographer and herself travelled to meet and photograph them. Since they don't have telephones, they went on spec. and the local Gardai showed the journalists where to find them.

She'd been to the North of Ireland for New Year's Eve to report on a new year from the peace line in Belfast.

And she'd been abroad - to America a few times, and to London several times, to interview celebrities, cover the World Cup and the Oscars, follow the Irish. It's a varied life, full of different things, she agrees. "You never know what the next day will bring."

And she writes an opinion column for Fridays. She's defended people's rights to take their own lives, and written about women who fall for the wrong type of men.

While her life might sound exciting and varied, being a freelance journalist has its downsides. She has to be constantly available. She's not a member of staff, she's on permanent call, and her work could end at any time. It's insecure, and competitive for many freelance journalists in the features world of Dublin journalism.

"I enjoy writing colour, and opinion, but it can be very difficult sometimes. With news, it's straightforward reporting of the facts. With colour, it has to be different every time."

Now a journalist for seven years, she believes persistence is one of the essential qualities of a good journalist.

"You need to be able to look at a lot of material and see the important stuff; you have to have an awful lot of common sense. You have to be able to know how people tick, and you have to be able to make people like you so they'll open up to you when you interview them. And you cannot be frightened of hostile reaction to opinion pieces or critical articles you might write."

And, of course, you need to be able to write on demand.

3 CHRONICLE OF THE COMMUNITY

The Provincial Press

The Irish provincial newspaper industry is currently facing the challenges posed by the development of local radio, the easy availability of more and more news, and the changing demands of a once loyal readership. While courts, sports and the goings-on at the local Urban District Council were once the staple diet of any local newspaper, the 1990s reader demands more.

However, the industry is generally coping well. Local newspapers are an integral and important part of the Irish media industry. The combination of a sharp business sense, where the newspaper often lives alongside a printing business, and a long-established relationship with its readers, has meant that the regional newspaper industry does not have to worry unduly about the future.

A recent survey by the Regional Newspaper Advertising Bureau claims that seventy-five per cent of all adults read a provincial newspaper each week.

The leaders in terms of readership are the *Kerryman*, the *Connacht Tribune*, the *Wexford People*, the *Limerick Leader*, and the *Clare Champion*, with the *Meath Chronicle*, the *Donegal Democrat*, the *Munster Express*, the *Leinster Express* and the *Dundalk Democrat* coming up close behind.

A LONG HISTORY

Many provincial papers, such as the *Nenagh Guardian*, the *Tuam Herald* and the *Sligo Champion* date back to the 1830's when there was a boom in newspaper publishing. Many towns boasted a number of titles. At one time Waterford had two evening papers.

Competition in the form of the national dailies *The Freeman's Journal* and *The Irish Times* forced the closure of a number of titles, as did the laws of libel.

The 1880s saw another boom in publishing, in many cases directly related to political developments. Many of the titles founded then – the *Midland Tribune*, the *Western People*, the *Southern Star*, the *Longford Leader*, the *Meath Chronicle*, the *Tipperary Nationalist* – were openly nationalist and Catholic, agitating for land reform.

The *Midland Tribune* was founded when the three Catholic curates in the Offaly town of Birr raised £1,000 to build an organ expressing Catholic and nationalist views. Similarly the *Southern Star* found priests involved in establishing an organ to counter the Protestant *Skibereen Eagle*.

And in the west, one of the first contributors to the *Western People* was Michael Davitt.

Competition became more keen in the early years of the new century with more titles appearing – the

Kerryman was born in Tralee in 1904. The first issue had ten pages and cost one penny.

The *Munster Express* was begun in 1907 and represented an amalgamation of all the publishing interests of Edward Walsh.

In 1902 a group of local businessmen, politicians and a solicitor founded the *Echo* and *South Leinster Times* and in 1904 the *Clare Champion* grew from the ashes of the *Clareman* – closed by a libel action.

Most of these titles still live today and have been joined by more. It is notable that they are still largely local or family-owned businesses.

The *Irish Independent* ventured into the world of provincial newspapers in 1968 with the acquisition of the *Drogheda Independent*. The *Kerryman* was next in 1972 and the Independent Group also owns the *People* Group of Wexford.

These are undoubtedly among the country's most successful titles with an average readership of about 30,000.

The provincial newspaper industry has not been threatened by the advent of local radio, with the two living successfully side by side, and indeed each using the other to advertise to readers and listeners. Provincial newspapers are also printing works and the greater profit is often on the printing side of the company. In this way the newspapers are secured by a purely commercial operation living under the same roof.

THE DUBLIN SCENE

The Dublin newspaper market is very different to its country cousin. Firstly it's dominated by freesheets, which can be irregular in their appearance and variable in quality.

However, there are a number which have shown themselves to be more durable.

The *Tallaght Echo* is a weekly tabloid and is not a freesheet. It sells into four areas which in terms of their population – easily matching and mostly exceeding the population of an average provincial town – among them Tallaght and Clondalkin.

The *Fingal Independent* sells into Dublin's northside and is part of the Drogheda Independent Group.

South News, formerly *Southside*, is one of the longest running, biggest circulation freesheets in the Dublin area. It is matched north of the river by the *Northside People*.

Lifetimes, produced by the *Irish Times*, distributes north and south of the Liffey and has probably the biggest circulation.

Other titles with local distribution are the *Fitzwilliam Post*, *South West Express*, and *News West*.

VICKI WELLER, EDITOR

Change is the Biggest Challenge

The announcement of a new editor for any publication is always news, but when the editor is a woman, it's a bigger story. In the more traditional world of provincial journalism, the appointment of a woman as editor is certainly unusual, but for Vicki Weller, it was in the blood.

Vicki was born into the business. Her father had worked in the *Leinster Leader* and she had always been interested in journalism as a career. Vicki grew up in the area, and went on to study English and German in UCD before but she began her journalistic career.

She started freelancing with the *Irish Independent*, based in Dublin, and stayed at this for two years until a job came up in the *Leinster Leader* as senior reporter. After 12 years as a reporter with the paper, she took over as Editor late last year succeeding Senan Carroll who had held that post for 35 years.

Married to a teacher and with two small children, Vicki recognises that while women are entering journalism in equal numbers to men, there is still a glass ceiling when it comes to promotion and places at the top. She feels that like other professions, women raising children as well as pursuing a career often choose not to seek promotion, simply because they cannot or do not want to take on more pressure in their lives. And she says there are still employers who do not believe that women are able to do the "big" job.

But the fact that of the nine reporting staff on the *Leader,* including herself, four are women, is evidence of the increasing numbers of women working in the media, including the provincial press.

She has taken up the challenge of ensuring that the *Leinster Leader*, currently with a readership of 15,500 a week, moves with the times and attracts a wider readership.

"The biggest challenge facing the industry is being able to adapt to change. People are becoming more and more visual and we have to be able to appeal to them. Using more photographs is one way – and breaking up the stories is another. Having acres of column inches on one story is no longer acceptable."

Just under the masthead on the front is evidence of how the Leader is widening its appeal.

"Schools – Bands go into Battle in Naas" and "Night Life – Pictures from the Cush Inn" sits beside "GAA – Big Game switched to Newbridge".

With more features and a Schools Page, where young readers are asked to contribute, and a regular profile as well as Fashion and Cookery columns, Entertainment and Music, the *Leader* is keeping up with the times.

Vicki has taken up the challenge of extending the

Vicki Weller of The Leinster Leader.   Photograph: Courtesy of the Leinster Leader.

Leader's circulation area to the growing towns of Leixlip, Celbridge and Maynooth in the north of the county, augmenting its existing base in the rest of Kildare, east Offaly and west Wicklow.

"North Kildare is difficult territory, because you are looking for readers among people who don't necessarily have links with Kildare. Many look more naturally to Dublin. So we are looking for those people who are putting down roots in the community and are interested in what's going on there."

A special issue is produced for North Kildare.

Vicki recognises that provincial papers are suffering like all other papers from a general drop in newspaper readership, but feels that the role of the newspaper in the local community is a very important one.

"Even in the United States, small communities produce their own newspapers. The paper is important to a community's sense of cohesion.

"But there is a battle ahead and we'll have to fight every inch of the way to maintain circulation. It's important to listen to the readers, respond to changes, keep the paper interesting.

"It's also important to stay on top of developments in new technology and to promote the paper in the community.

"Keeping up with change is the biggest challenge we face for the future."

PROVINCIAL PAPERS CIRCULATION FIGURES FOR 1994

Title	Circulation	Title	Circulation
Anglo-Celt	15,888	Meath Chronicle	19,635
Dundalk Argus	8,250	Munster Express	18,500
Clare Champion	19,800	Nationalist & Leinster Times	17,170
Connacht Tribune	27,614	Nationalist Newspaper	15,578
Connacht Sentinel	6,160	Nenagh Guardian	7,702
Connaught Telegraph	12,000	Northern Standard	13,500
Donegal Democrat	19,177	People Group*	35,950
Donegal Peoples Press	9,217	Roscommon Herald	16,000
Drogheda Independent	13,255	Sligo Champion	16,390
Dundalk Democrat	18,000	Southern Star	16,250
Kerryman	33,392	Tipperary Star	10,434
Kilkenny People	16,687	Tuam Herald	10,800
Leinster Express	18,239	Waterford News & Star	15,500
Leinster Leader	15,450	Western People	24,000
Limerick Leader	26,249	Westmeath Examiner	13,295
Limerick Chronicle	6,941	Westmeath Offaly Independent	13,463
Mayo News	11,500		

* People Group = 5 papers.

Source: The Provincial Newspapers Association of Ireland.

4 NO MORE HARD QUESTIONS

Magazines

Probably the most notable development in the Irish magazine market in the last decade has been the demise of the current affairs magazine.

There has also been the considerable success in Ireland of one of the most recent recruits to the magazine market – the *Big Issues*, sold on the street by the homeless and unemployed and based on an idea which has also succeeded in Britain.

But the current affairs magazine, once a major feature of Irish journalism, has faded. For a brief few years in the first half of the 1980's, some of the country's best writers and enquiring minds filled the columns of *Magill, Status, Aspect* and briefly, *In Dublin*. Before then, *Hibernia* had asked the hard questions.

The Irish media industry has changed, and it is worth remembering that investigative journalism is both time-consuming and expensive, whether it's being done by a newspaper, magazine or a broadcasting organisation.

It is also worth noting that the stories which have shaken the Irish political firmament in recent times – the Beef Industry exposé, and the Fr Brendan Smyth affair – were both first reported by the British media.

This is not to say that there aren't good writers around. The standard of reporting and broadcasting in Ireland is as good as any other country, but the focus has shifted elsewhere.

From time to time the columns of *Hot Press*, the music magazine, produces the type of writing which reminds the reader of the golden days of Colm Toibín, Gene Kerrigan, Mary Raftery, Michael Higgins, and John Waters.

Business and Finance has carried on, but *In Dublin* is purely a listings magazine now. *Magill* is closed, and *Hibernia* experienced just a brief revival as *New Hibernia*, in the 80s.

WOMEN READERS

On the non-current affairs side, the magazine publishing industry is well with a good market for Irish-produced women's magazines in particular.

With sales of 120,000 per issue, the *RTE Guide* is Ireland's largest selling magazine, outstripping its rivals and turning in a healthy profit for RTE's own company, Commercial Enterprises.

This compares to average monthly sales of between 21,000 and 23,000 for Ireland's three women's monthlies, *Image, U* and *IT*, while the weekly *Woman's Way* remains the biggest seller among the highly competitive women's market, with a circulation figure of 68,000. Smurfit Publications dominates the magazine market, with *Woman's Way*, *U Magazine* and *IT* in its stable.

NICHE AND TRADE MAGAZINES

Journals which act as communications networks for business associations, professional bodies and institutes form the solid core of the trade magazine industry in Ireland. Specialist journals and periodicals are also an important and growing part of this industry and with developments in desktop publishing and printing technology, production has become cheaper and the magazines themselves much more attractive.

Irish Brides, Health and Safety, Management, Hotel and Catering Review, Food Ireland, Checkout, Irish Medical News – these are just some of the large list of trade and professional magazines published here.

The big players in the trade magazine industry are Jemma Publications, Jude Publications, Tara publications, MAC Publishing, Oisin and Dyflin Publications. Each publishing house is responsible for a number of titles.

Specialised publishers include Roundhall Press, which produces legal reports, books and magazines for the legal profession.

Many professional and private organisations produce their own magazines, such as *Consumer Choice* or *An Bord Altranais News*.

Magazines vary from the subscription-only, to the generally-sold, but are characterised by being directed at specific target audiences and often professional groups i.e. the *Irish Doctor*, the *Engineers Journal*, the *Irish Printer* and the *Garda Journal*.

They are also characterised by heavy advertising, and in some cases, by press releases repeated word for word, or "puff" editorial copy, obviously influenced by contributing advertisers.

Trade magazines can be a good opening for a trainee journalist or a freelance journalist who is able to turn that "puff" into well-written, easily-read copy.

MAURA O'KIELY, EDITOR

Sex, Health and Giveaways

There are no knitting patterns in *U* magazine.

Current editor, thirty-something-year-old Maura O'Kiely admits she's not the knitting type, and that the regular knitting pattern was dropped when she took over. But the change also has a lot to do with how the magazine's target audience sees itself. They're not the knitting type either.

Aimed at the 18 to 35 age group, predominantly female reader, the *U* magazine agenda is based on sex, health, personalities, fashion and beauty.

Maura O'Kiely is close to her readers – so close indeed that she often writes back to those readers who contact her with their reaction to a piece in the magazine or with their own personal stories. Sometimes those stories become magazine pieces – but only with the permission of the person themselves.

Letters provide a sounding board, and often ideas for material. Other sources of ideas are the creative minds of contributors, daily papers, press releases, or the storyline on Glenroe.

Her own role in the magazine is one of traffic and quality control. "Three quarters of my day is spent subbing and re-writing copy," she says. "I'm also responsible for commissioning, picture sourcing, caption writing, headline writing, and getting the cover together – six weeks in advance of publication."

Maura's own journalistic career has been dominated by "womens' writing". As part of the NIHE Dublin journalism diploma, Maura did a placement on *Woman's Way*, another of the successful Smurfit stable. She spent a number of years as a freelance contributor not only to the "womens' mags" but also on the national dailies and Sundays. She drifted into fashion writing and became Fashion Editor at *Woman's Way* before coming into *U* as Assistant Editor in 1991, and Editor shortly afterwards.

Maura sees the magazine tracking the changes among her reader age group in modern Ireland. When the magazine began in 1979, it had a much greyer, staid look. Now AIDS as a health issue for women is a big story and the letters Maura gets tell her of a generation that wants more out of life and is prepared to demand it.

The high gloss, high colour look of the *U* magazine of the 1990s with its high style, sophisticated fashion spreads are pitched to compete with the glossies from England – *Cosmo*, *Elle*, *Vogue*, and of course, in a league all its own – *Hello*.

Editor of U Magazine, Maura O'Kiely.   Photograph: Courtesty of U Magazine.

5 FROM THE MARKETS TO THE MEDICS

Specialist Press

One of the most striking aspects of journalism is its diversity: for every Charlie Bird or Veronica Guerin, there is a travel writer, a radio sports reporter or an agriculture specialist; dozens and dozens of journalists work in the area that is not general news i.e. features, profiles, personal columns, reviews, supplements.

This chapter deals with these areas: the specialist media. As the world of information expands, the media has responded by diversifying the subjects within its pages, hence the growing demand for specialist journalists.

WHERE SPECIALIST JOURNALISTS BELONG

The main newspapers and broadcast organisations have their own specialist journalists; many edit and write their own supplements and are well known outside their field. They have their own columns; some are experts in their fields.

As broadcast technology brings more and more instant news to people, the print media are relying on specialist journalists who bring the insight and detail to a comprehensive coverage of a breaking news story in a way that the rapid turnover of television and radio news doesn't.

HOW DO PEOPLE BECOME SPECIALIST JOURNALISTS?

Many journalists become specialists as a natural progression from being general reporters, and who show a flair for a particular area. Many general reporters have no specific training to cover areas like finance or agriculture, but they have the ability to translate technical and complicated information into plain English for their readers.

WHAT AREAS DO SPECIALIST JOURNALISTS COVER?

The following are the main specialist areas of journalism in the print and broadcast media:

- Politics
- Finance

- Sport
- Investigative
- Agriculture
- Crime/Security
- Property
- Environment
- Industrial Relations
- Education/Social Affairs
- Medical/Science
- Entertainment/Arts/Music
- Books
- Fashion and Beauty/Lifestyles
- Travel and Holidays
- Foreign
- Food and Drink

WHERE DO SPECIALIST JOURNALISTS WORK?

Newsrooms

Within newsrooms, beside the general reporters, specialists in news-related subjects cover the ground of their own patch: they closely follow developments in their areas, keep in touch with their contacts, provide the news editor with ideas for news stories and the features department with background analyses and interviews. Many exclusive stories in newspapers come from specialists digging in their own territories.

Features Departments

Newspapers have become more wide-ranging in their coverage of specialised subjects; less and less news is replaced by more and more features, written in the most part by specialist journalists. The middle section of a daily paper consists of Arts coverage, Business and Finance, Sports and Lifestyles articles. Many have their own separate pages appearing on a weekly basis, and in weekend sections and columns.

Supplements

News gathering operations have broadened their coverage of many aspects of society - the *Irish Independent* and *The Irish Times*, for example, have almost daily specialised supplements covering different areas - Sports, Agriculture, Education, Property and Business - which provide detailed news and background to their worlds.

Trade Magazines and Journals

More and more professions are producing specialist papers for their own members - accountants, doctors, farmers, engineers, for example, all have their own publications aimed specifically at their attention. The *Farmers Journal* and the *Irish Medical Times* are good examples.

THE GROUND COVERED

Politics

Political correspondents, political reporters, colour writers, and Dail reporters are all specialists in political journalism. Mostly they are based at Leinster House, where they have a separate press room, and where they cover the daily goings-on in national political life. Political correspondents, who are the most senior and specialised of the group, have access to the party leaders and senior politicians; they travel with the leaders on their trips, and get off-the-record briefings from senior political sources. (See profile of Brian Dowling page 119.)

Finance

From accountants to economists to people with little qualifications, finance is a huge area in journalism, covering everything from Government spending, to personal finance columns to the Stock Exchange, to inside stories on the investments and fortunes of individual companies. With a number of separate pages on a daily basis, and often a separate supplement, finance journalism has an influential role; much of the best investigative journalism of recent years has come from this area.

Agriculture

From mart reports to intensive Brussels negotiations, agricultural journalists cover a huge variety of subjects from animal husbandry to the latest IFA presidential election. In a country with such a big agricultural industry, farming stories are rarely out of the news, and all the national newspapers have correspondents and special supplements.

Crime/Security

This area comes into its own at times of big robberies and high profile shootings or kidnappings. A difficult area to report, many journalists rely on off-the-record briefings, building up confidential and close contacts in the world of the criminal, and the police and watching closely the internal dynamics of its organisations.

Property

From the hugely successful supplements in the daily newspapers, to the occasional front page story about the latest successful property deal, this area ranges from high finance, to social reporting. (See profile of Cliodhna O'Donoghue in this chapter.)

The Environment

A growing area, made all the bigger by the widespread awareness of the Green movement, and the greater interest in environmental issues, it covers everything from threats to the national heritage, to local disputes over land use, to legal disputes and oil spillages.

Industrial Relations

Industrial disputes loom large in this area, as well as analysis of complex and often detailed trade relations. Everything from the "downsizing" of large employers to the role of trade unions in the modern world, this area also covers the world of the workplace and the impact of technology on future jobs. (See profile of Tim Hastings in this chapter.)

Education/Social Affairs

Dominated by the world of schools, legislation covering education and the workings of teacher unions, the Education Correspondent must also be able to understand exam results, careers and politics.

Social Affairs, often covered by the same correspondent, deals with issues relating to poverty, the unemployed and the disadvantaged groups in society.

Medical/Science

Everything from medical politics, rows in hospitals to the latest treatment for varicose veins, newspaper coverage tends to veer towards the political and trade union aspects of the medical world. There is a thriving market in trade magazines for the large number of workers in the health service.

Entertainment/Music/ Cinema/ the Arts

Often with its own section in daily newspapers, as well as a big industry, this area covers a wide range of subjects from social gossip about film and pop stars, to reviews and coverage of concerts and events, as well as the news of developments in the arts. A large number of part-time specialist journalists contribute columns and reviews to the specialist sections on these subjects.

Books

Weekend sections of newspapers give over a large amount of space to reviews, news and coverage of the writing world. Many of the contributors are themselves writers.

Fashion and Beauty/ Lifestyles

A growing area, with popular appeal, covering everything from the latest fashions, to the latest diet. Women's health is a big subject and women's magazines are a large industry in this area. Most newspapers have their own fashion editors, who bring a weekly opinion on the latest trends from Paris or Grafton Street.

Lifestyles includes everything from health to interior design and is a growing area within newspapers and magazines.

Travel and Holidays

Although there are very few specialist travel writers, the weekend supplements of newspapers, as well as sections in magazines, are where these journalists reside. With some emphasis on the "consumer" side, giving the latest trends and prices, this area also covers developments in the travel trade, and involves many journeys abroad.

Investigative Journalism

Fewer and fewer newspapers are devoting full-time journalists to this area, mainly because it is costly and investigations can take a long time. (See profile of Veronica Guerin in this chapter.) Often journalists from other areas are drafted into big investigations, having unearthed the story themselves. In recent years the finance area of journalism has dug up some significant business scandals, and it was through her agricultural journalism that researcher Susan O'Keeffe tracked the fortunes of Larry Goodman for her

"World in Action" exposé of the practices in the Irish beef industry.

Currently no newspaper has a team of investigative reporters like the famed "Insight" team on the *Sunday Times* in the Seventies, and *Magill* magazine, formerly an outlet for investigative journalism, is no longer published.

Sports

This is a significant area of journalism, comprising several pages in the daily, and evening papers, a wide range of specialist magazines and newspapers, as well as huge television and radio coverage.

Sports journalism in newspapers has become more column-based and analysis has replaced straight reporting of events as the broadcast media has taken over the almost instantaneous reporting of daily and weekend events, especially results.

Sports journalism sometimes leaks onto the front news page when a leading personality, or a sport takes on more mainstream appeal. A huge growth area in journalism, and the only qualification is: an interest in sport and the ability to describe it. (See profile of Martin Breheny on following page.)

Foreign

Despite the broader coverage by newspapers of world events, foreign correspondents are expensive to maintain and insure, and more and more newspapers are relying on local reporters to file copy on a freelance basis. Quality daily newspapers employ considerable numbers of journalists in their foreign offices; many go abroad for a few years, to return to domestic newsrooms and other specialisms.

Other

There are other specialist areas: gardening, for example, and other leisure activities are getting more and more space in the media. It is generally qualified gardeners who write columns and articles in newspapers giving advice, and answering readers' queries.

New Technology is a growing area of specialist journalism, with the development of a greater range of computers and communications equipment. Much of the journalism in this area covers the latest developments, as well as information on how to buy and use the latest gadget, or how to sign onto the Internet.

The Media itself is becoming another specialist area, with the growth in media studies, analysis of media coverage of stories, and the reporting on personnel changes.

Martin Breheny at his desk in the Sunday Press.   Photograph: Courtesy of the Sunday Press.

MARTIN BREHENY, SPORTS JOURNALIST

From Air Traffic Controller to GAA - Keeping your Eye on the Ball

Martin Breheny smiles when he talks about his job, the GAA correspondent for the *Sunday Press*.

"I am paid to do the job that most men at least, would want to have - going to matches and writing about them afterwards, and meeting the sports people and getting to know how it all works. What I call 'work' is most people's hobby."

A passionate interest in sport is the essential requirement of a good sports journalist, believes Martin, who's also Deputy Sports News Editor and Boxing Correspondent for the *Press* group of newspapers.

He got into journalism through an unusual route; he was training to be an Air Traffic Controller and decided it didn't suit him. He moved to working in insurance - "all the time bombarding the *Tuam Herald* and editor Jarlath Burke with stories and ideas".

He was 22 when the editor gave him a job as a general news and sports reporter. "Provincial journalism is a great training, it gives a good grounding in the fundamentals of journalism," he says.

He thinks young aspiring journalists should get a strong grounding in the basics of news reporting. "Now everyone wants to be an analyst - but at the end of the day they're called "newspapers" because they carry the news. I bemoan the death of the verb in journalism."

He believes luck plays a vital role in a journalist's career - and being in the right place at the right time. "When I came into the Press, I covered boxing when a vacancy arose, and then there was the Olympics in 1980 and I got sent to Moscow.

He was also in place for the Barry McGuigan phenomenon and covered his World Title fight in 1985, and he covered the 1988 Olympic Games.

But like other aspects of journalism, you can get cynical and stale in sports journalism too.

"It's easy to see a match as just another game, but big events like a major championship match take you through that phase."

And there's a danger of becoming complacent, of rowing in behind the establishment - "becoming one of them and having a comfortable life." He has a reputation as a critic of the GAA hierarchy. "I get criticism from them for my attitudes, but you can't be uncritical. You know it's their job to keep things from you, it's your job to find them out. You have to be constantly aware of this, but if you know your subject well enough you will be sure of your ground."

VERONICA GUERIN, INVESTIGATIVE JOURNALIST

A Journalist Who Doesn't Give Up

On crutches, and limping, Veronica Guerin reaches for the phone that is constantly ringing. Her home is her office.

Since she was shot in the leg at her home following her stories into publicity-shy Dublin criminals, the *Sunday Independent's* Veronica Guerin has become a recognised public face.

"It's a bit of disadvantage to be recognised now," she admits. The people she meets and talks to don't always want to be recognised or noticed.

Not many investigative journalists has been shot in Ireland for what they had written. But not many journalists in Ireland are like Veronica Guerin.

With no formal training as a journalist, she says she cannot write and finds it very difficult to put her information in a readable form.

She tracked down Bishop Eamon Casey to a remote village in central America, and got a series of exclusive and revealing interviews after going to the country on a whim.

An accountant by training, she became a journalist by accident when she met *Sunday Business Post* editor Damien Kiberd.

Unlike most freelance journalists, she had the financial independence to concentrate on investigations - a time-consuming exercise in digging out information, meeting contacts, sometimes following up dead-end leads.

Time and Tenacity

"To be an investigative journalist, you need time, and anyone who works in a newsroom as a general reporter doesn't have that. Sometimes I will work three to four weeks non-stop to get a story, meeting people morning, noon and night. People won't talk to you on the phone, you need to meet them, often outside office hours."

She spent six months on her first big investigation - fraudulent practices in an Aer Lingus Holidays subsidiary. "Digging, digging, digging" is her description of her work methods. Tenacity and patience are the central requirements of getting to the heart of a story.

She moved to the *Sunday Tribune* in 1993, and after the Eamon Casey stories, she transferred to the *Sunday Independent*, where she began crime investigations. The deadlines of Sunday papers suit her methods.

"There are two ways of doing crime stories," she said. "You can investigate the Gardai or you can investigate the criminals. I decided to try and gain the trust and confidence of the criminals, and that's how I got my stories. I wrote two letters a day for six weeks to Martin Cahill before he decided to talk to me."

She works completely on her own, mostly from home, sending in her copy by modem from her computer; she communicates with *Sunday Independent* News Editor Willie Kealy by phone.

"It's a big advantage. You are your own boss, you do your own thing. If you are working on a story that needs to be investigated, then you cannot pick the days and the hours that you will work. I wouldn't want a routine.

"There is nobody else doing what I am doing. The awful thing about Irish journalism now is that the *Sunday Independent* is the only paper that can afford to employ someone who's working on investigations full-time. Other journalists are uncovering stories, but they do not have the luxury that I have to work on them full-time."

When she first started writing stories on a freelance basis for the *Sunday Business Post*, she thought it was a simple job, this journalism.

"I said at the time, this is easy money. Little did I know!

"I have been asking myself since I got shot - is it worth it? Will I change? What am I doing it for? I think I do it because I love it and I find it fulfilling. As soon as I get bored I'll move on to something else."

CLIODHNA O'DONOGHUE, PROPERTY EDITOR

The Bricks and Mortar of Property Journalism

One of the biggest stories that Cliodhna O'Donoghue broke in the *Irish Independent* was the involvement of Michael Smurfit and Dermot Desmond in the Johnson Mooney and O'Brien site in Ballsbridge in Dublin.

Her article was the beginning of a major controversy over Telecom Eireann's purchase of the site at a time when its chairman had a financial interest in it. It was several years before an official inquiry proved her story to be correct.

Property journalism is not always about the latest style of kitchen in Dublin townhouse developments.

From the mundane to the money

Property journalism ranges from the exciting to the mundane, and requires an ability to see the interesting in the ordinary, and find a story in a mound of technical information.

But after five years in a demanding and pressuring job, Cliodhna O'Donoghue clearly loves it and relishes its variety.

As the editor of the most widely-read property supplement in the country- Friday's "Independent Property" - she chooses the houses people go to look at; her opinion can make or break a development, and people in the business follow her stories closely.

From 32 to 40 pages every Friday, she is assisted by two journalists in writing three or four stories for each page of copy, as well as a lead story, editing copy, and choosing photographs to go with the text.

A minimum of three stories, and at least two houses on each page is the rule, over eight to 10 pages- that's about 30 new stories a week. Cliodhna and her colleagues spend a lot of time on the phone to their contacts - their copy must be completely up to date for the Friday readership. They are in regular contact with estate agents, builders, developers and public relations companies.

For the Wednesday Commercial Property page, there's a list of areas to cover: Shops, Pubs, Industrial, Offices, Developments, Investments as well as a lead and off-lead story.

Not to mention side stories of reports and analysis.

Filling the Gap

Seeing a gap in the market brought Cliodhna O'Donoghue from her initial job in marketing to property journalism.

Property Editor, Cliodhna O'Donoghue, at her desk.   Photograph: Kate Horgan.

She had founded a property magazine for the Irish Auctioneers and Valuers Institute, recognising a need in the market for features and information on a wide range of property-related matters from licensing laws to property deals.

But she's not confined to the Property pages of the *Independent*. Because she is in constant contact with the industry, she has exclusive stories that make the front page of the newspaper about the latest investments or property deals.

"There's quite a bit of crossover into news," she says. "Especially on the big financial deals. Sometimes I have a story that just cannot wait until Friday."

"There's a massive amount of work," she says. "As well as the pages, I attend two to three seminars a week, and I go to launches, to conferences and to lunches, to meet people and hear what's happening in the business."

Becoming the Expert

There are advantages to being a specialist journalist.

"You get to know your subject very well," she says. "A day-to-day reporter cannot do that.

"In my case I developed a strong interest in the topics, I love to hear about the intricacies of the deals, and now I can almost guess their complexities.

"The downsides of being a specialist is that you miss being in the centre a big news story that breaks because it's not your area," she says.

Being your own boss can be an advantage, but "you can't lean on anyone else. You must be there if the story is breaking. People look to me for contacts, for information".

BROADCASTING

Introduction

Irish Broadcasting is going through a period of change. Local radio has changed the landscape for listeners throughout the country, breaking the monopoly held for so long by RTE and denting its listenership figures. And although RTE maintains its dominant position as a national broadcaster, it may yet have to change and adapt in the face of competition from an alternative national station.

Legislation designed to develop an independent programme-making industry has injected major funding into the sector – but the decisions on what programmes are made still lies in the hands of RTE.

The national station dominates the industry. With 1916 employees, it is the largest employer in the Irish media industry, running the two most popular radio stations, RTE Radio One and 2FM and the only two Irish television stations, RTE One and Network 2.

But change is ahead. The current Minister responsible for Broadcasting, Michael D. Higgins, has published a Green Paper on the future of Broadcasting in Ireland. This is a discussion document which will ultimately lead to new legislation to regulate broadcasting in Ireland.

Among the most significant of the possibilities looked at is the merger of the current RTE Authority with the Independent Radio and Television Commission into a "Superauthority" which would assume overall responsibility for the policy and regulatory functions associated with broadcasting. This might include, in the future, responsibility for the development of an independent alternative news and current affairs service, run on a commercial basis, independent of RTE; this could include a national radio news service, available to non-RTE stations.

Another proposal which would also signal major change within RTE is the creation of an entirely commercial transmission operation, independent of RTE, which would provide technical services to all broadcasters, including RTE and the independent stations. Currently RTE manages the transmission system. Making it independent would, according to the Green Paper, allow RTE to concentrate on its core function – programme making.

The Green Paper also poses the possibility of 2FM Radio being turned into an independent, commercial operation, and suggests that with the development of local radio, Cork Local Radio as run by RTE is an anomaly. If these proposals were acted upon, RTE would be a radically changed organisation.

RTE could still face competition on the television front. Despite the setbacks faced by TV3, the IRTC still hopes for the development of a third, independent, TV channel.

Competition from British channels with much more resources, and from satellite channels, has not put much of a dent in RTE's dominant position with Irish audiences. But the increasing availability of same-language television stations through satellite broadcasting will put further pressure on what is, in European terms, a very small television station.

Ultimately, RTE's public service broadcasting remit will have to be adapted if its requirement to remain commercial and profitable is to be maintained.

6 THE VOICE OF THE NATION

RTE Radio

RADIO ONE

RTE Radio One has come a long way since it opened nearly 70 years ago.

The first national radio station began transmission on 1 January 1926, and it was then called 2RN. The radio station was based in small studios in Little Denmark Street off Henry Street, in Dublin's city centre.

The Government had decided that broadcasting in Ireland should be run by the state as a public service medium and would be financed by a combination of licence fees and the broadcasting of advertisements. At that time, people with receivers could hear the BBC and continental stations.

On that first night in 1926, apart from a speech by Douglas Hyde, the founder of the Gaelic League, the schedule consisted mostly of music and singing; that soon changed.

Within a year, a basic news service had been set up, and programmes on farming, literary matters and the weather forecast were incorporated.

But it was the broadcast of the All-Ireland hurling semi-final between Galway and Kilkenny in August of 1926 that showed the possibilities of a mass radio audience, and it soon became a popular medium in rural Ireland.

In 1932, the station changed its name to Radio Eireann; it had moved studios to the General Post Office in Henry Street in 1928 and remained there until 1974 when it transferred to the new, bigger radio centre in Donnybrook, on Dublin's southside.

Television came on air in 1961, and in 1966, the title of the complete service was changed to Radio Telefís Eireann (RTE).

In 1960, Radio One went from being a direct State service within the Department of Posts and Telegraphs to becoming a statutory corporation, created along with television under the Broadcasting Authority Act, 1960. This established an RTE Authority of nine members, appointed by the Government. The Director General of RTE heads the organisation.

FROM GAYBO TO THE NATIONAL CONCERT HALL: THE MODERN SERVICE

Nowadays RTE Radio bears little resemblance to the small station in Henry Street.

As the national broadcasting organisation, its radio service is comprehensive.

As well as Radio One, there is 2FM, FM3 Music and Radio na Gaeltachta, as well as Cork Local Radio.

The RTE Complex.   Photograph: Courtesy of RTE.

- Radio One is the national service, providing a comprehensive news service in English and Irish, wide sports coverage, current affairs, features, drama, religion and music, as well as a broad range of minority programmes. It is widely available on medium wave from a number of transmitters, as well as the FM band.

- 2FM is the popular music channel, formed in 1979. Catering mainly for a younger audience, it is also available on the medium wave. With its own news service and sports coverage, it is a 24-hour station.

- Raidio na Gaeltachta is the national broadcasting service in the Irish language, for the Gaeltacht areas, and is available on medium wave and nationwide on FM. It was founded in 1972 as a service for Irish speakers and the Gaeltachts, and has expanded its service in recent years to 12 hours a day. It provides a news and current affairs service, sports, Irish music, drama and debate. Headquartered in Connemara, it also has studios in Donegal, Kerry, Dublin and Mayo.

- FM3 Music is primarily a classical music station, sharing the same wavelength as Raidio na Gaeltachta on the FM band, transmitting in the early mornings, evenings and weekends. It offers orchestral concerts, opera, chamber, choral music and European music festivals.

- Cork Local Radio transmits to the Cork area as a local news and current affairs service for 6 hours a day on Cork 89FM and the local medium wave.

THE ORCHESTRA

RTE Radio is the largest and one of the most important patrons of music in the country. Since 1947, it has maintained orchestras, on the BBC tradition of public service broadcasting. RTE employs more than 130 full-time musicians and many more on a freelance basis.

Its orchestras are: The National Symphony Orchestra and the RTE Concert Orchestra.

There is also the Philharmonic Choir, the RTE Chamber Choir, Cór na nOg, and the RTE Vanburgh String Quartet, which is based in Cork.

LISTENERSHIP FIGURES – THE TOP RADIO PROGRAMMES

The combined RTE radio stations, according to 1994 listenership surveys, show that nationally, RTE Radio has a 59% share of daytime listening every weekday.

Over one million people listen to RTE Radio One each weekday; 2FM has almost three quarters of a million listeners, with a 21% share. In Dublin, RTE Radio One share is strong, due mainly to the lack of an alternative talk radio station for the capital.

These are the listenership figures for RTE's top radio programmes for 1994:

- Morning Ireland: 644,000
- Gay Byrne Show 556,000

- News at One 432,000
- Liveline 417,000
- Gerry Ryan Show (on 2FM) 403,000
- Pat Kenny Show 389,000

Following a strengthening of the RTE Radio One schedule in the 80s to counter the arrival of Century Radio, four main personalities have dominated RTE Radio: Gay Byrne, Pat Kenny, Marion Finucane and Gerry Ryan. All command huge audiences, in daytime and early afternoon programmes, complemented by strong listenership for the morning news programme, Morning Ireland, and the lunchtime News at One.

On 2FM, the morning Gerry Ryan Show has a huge lead over other programmes on that station.

In the afternoons, evenings and weekends, Radio One is losing audiences to the local radio stations, and is failing to attract younger audiences, who are listening in even greater numbers to the other RTE radio station, 2FM.

2 FM: THE YOUNGER STATION

Formed in 1979 to counter the then burgeoning pirate radio pop music stations, what was then RTE Radio Two rapidly developed into a slick, commercial pop music station. As the pirate stations were taken off the air by legislation and new independent stations, 2FM

gained a successful national audience, and now has a market share of 20%, and is holding its own in Dublin against the commercial stations there, 98FM and 104FM.

When it first started, the station had a much more diverse music policy, including music programmes with jazz, blues, and folk. As commercial competition became more severe, 2FM replaced this policy with a more middle-of-the-road music policy of contemporary, current and oldies, aimed at the under 35s during the day, and the under 20s in the evenings.

2FM is now a 24-hour station, with a wide range of presenters, a Roadcaster which travels the country, live and studio recordings of new bands, a studio in Tallaght in Dublin, and a huge audience in the morning with its only talk radio programme, the Gerry Ryan Show.

Since the beginning, the channel has had its own news service, 2FM News, which is based in the RTE Newsroom.

OTHER RTE SERVICES

Outside the broadcasting services provided in radio and television, RTE also has a number of other commercial activities.

AERTEL is the free teletext service, providing news and information on programmes, finance and consumer information, on domestic televisions in over 300,000 homes throughout the country.

The RTE Guide, contains complete television and radio listings for the week, as well as satellite channels, and background features on programmes and personalities. It is the biggest selling magazine in Ireland selling over 180,000 copies per week.

RTE Radio can also be heard by telephone throughout the Republic, Northern Ireland, Britain and Brussels, and the United States by dialling various phone numbers. A news and sports service is available, with Radio One available in Brussels.

Both of these services are very popular with Irish communities abroad.

RTE ABROAD

For several years now, RTE radio has been available through satellite technology throughout the EC countries, and in North America. This is done via the Astra satellite, which carries RTE Radio at a frequency of 7.56MHz, and can be found on the MTV channel on the television, and relayed through the TV's speakers.

KEVIN HEALY, HEAD OF RADIO

The job of the Director of Radio Programmes in RTE, Kevin Healy, is to predict the pace and nature of the huge changes radio in Ireland is now going through.

One the one hand, he is in a strong position. RTE Radio is performing well against the opposition, and retains an almost monopolistic position over radio.

It holds the highest audiences in its news and morning and early afternoon programmes, and it is preparing for the arrival of the successor to Century Radio, the first national commercial radio station. A new commercial rival to RTE Radio will soon be on the air, and Healy doesn't want to give away any of his audience.

He is not complacent. He's aware of the ageing profile of the Radio One audience, and the fact that the new national station will be chasing that 25-40 age group.

Audience ratings matter. They determine the advertising revenue, vital for RTE, which gets 60% of its income from commercial revenue.

"We are a public service broadcaster, but we're required to be commercial as well."

But he does predict "radical changes" in the Radio One programme schedule over the next few years, to counter the ageing profile. "We are losing our core audience." A radio review group has just finalised its report; changes are expected.

Outside the high profile morning schedule, RTE Radio One still caters for minorities. "The audience is like a cake with 20 slices, each one different. There are minority audiences, and I think we have to serve them as the national broadcaster. The challenge is to provide a mix, and to provide a very strong public service.

"Radio One is world class, one of the best radio stations in the world," he says.

He's responsible for other stations too within the radio network. Raidio na Gaeltachta has expanded its hours and FM3 is sharing its wavelength.

"FM3 listeners don't like that. I would like to have an Arts and Culture channel, a separate one for those listeners."

"I would love to see that coming in. It is an exciting possibility. Not like the Classic FM station in Britain. This would cater for a wider brief, e.g. The Arts Show would go out five nights a week, a chance to repeat good documentaries. Do drama, educational programming for schools, and have no news or current affairs on it at all."

A DAY IN THE LIFE OF...

THE 24TH YEAR OF THE GAY BYRNE RADIO PROGRAMME.

THURSDAY, 16 FEBRUARY 1995

7.30am Producer Cliodna O'Flynn makes a decision to scrap the planned programme of the day and replace it with a reaction programme to last night's trouble at the Ireland-England soccer game in Lansdowne Road rugby grounds. The planned programme - a special on the Famine - is postponed to another day.

   In the Gay Byrne Show office in the Radio Centre, four producers and a researcher are already working on the programme. Downstairs, the presenter is in Studio 7 reading the newspapers and preparing his notes.

8.00am The News and "Morning Ireland" are on in the background. Producer Yetti Redmond is taking a call from an angry soccer fan. Cliodna tells researcher Barbara Jordan, "We're going wall-to-wall soccer". Everyone will be needed to take phone calls. Barbara is looking for one of the Irish players.

8.30am Yetti tells Cliodna her caller was "in the middle of the yobs" on the West Stand, and gives Cliodna some typed notes. Joe Duffy is down at the East Wall where the supporters are catching the boat. The programme will take two callers from the public first, then Joe, decides Cliodna.

8.40am Producer Mary Campbell takes a call from a member of the public about the match.

8.50am Barbara Jordan talks to soccer journalist George Byrne on the phone. She takes notes; he agrees to take a call.

9.00am The News and It Says in the Papers can be heard on the speakers in the control room of Studio 5; sound operator Sean Campbell is in place; Alan Halford is ready to play discs, and broadcasting assistant Mary Martin is phoning the first caller; she sits beside Cliodna with four telephone lines on her telephone machine in front of her. The desk area is cramped.

9.05am Gay rehearses his first script, his table a mixture of pieces of letters, newspaper cuttings, and information. People come in and out of the control room with notes, calls and news.

9.07am The red light goes on in studio, Gay puts on headphones. Cliodna's phone rings - Barbara has another good caller who's rung in upstairs. "I'll take him second or third."

9.11am The signature tune is begun. Gay starts with the story of the *Star* photographer Neil Fraser, injured by a flying missile at the match, and reads comments from the newspaper coverage.

9.17am Caller Jim Gleeson is put up on air, the man in the middle of the yobs.

9.20am Barbara brings down typed details of George Byrne's comments, and his telephone number. Broadcasting assistants bring in the first comments from the phone-in line. Cliodna picks some of them to call back, others to read out. She adds notes to some of them for Gay.

9.24am The second caller is put on air, and Joe Duffy rings through. "We'll do you next," Mary Martin says.

9.37am "Joe, where are you?" asks Gay. Joe on a mobile phone describes the scene at the Irish Ferries terminal, with "120 incredibly subdued" fans. While Joe is talking, Cliodna chooses the next caller, Bob from Liverpool who rang in upstairs.

9.42am Bob tells Gay of his anger at his fellow countrymen.

9.43am George Burns is on the air. Cliodhna asks Sean to merge the two commercial breaks into one. Barbara has another good caller on the line.

9.55am Gay reads a few cards from listeners, and does a question on the Irish Ferries competition. He talks up to the News at 10 o'clock with Emer O'Kelly, who reads from a studio in a different building.

10.01am Barbara Jordan has contacted David Kelly, the Irish player who scored the first goal of the match. He discusses the match with Gay.

Cliodna chooses callers from the comments taken by the telephonists from a room up the corridor from the studio; she brings notes and other comments into Gay in the studio.

10.15am Gay talks to a caller. Cliodna chooses another.

10.20am Cliodna rings the office upstairs asking if someone can track down the little blonde boy whose face appeared on all the television coverage last night. A caller has rung giving his father's name.

10.25am Gay gives a hand signal. Commercial break.

10.35am Mary keeps a line clear so that Inspector Brian Drew of the Football Intelligence Unit in London can ring through.

Upstairs the phones are hopping. Sky TV and ITN are looking for the name of the blonde boy.

10.38am Caller Emma Kennedy from Manchester discusses the city with Gay, and then he takes a call from Peter in Wolverhampton. Noise levels in the control room rise.

10.50am There's one commercial break left. Sean checks that the signature tune is prepared to run at 10.58.50 and watches the clock.

10.55am The last commercial break is played. Two callers are on the line waiting to talk.

11.58am Gay reads out some of the comments - all of them about the incidents. The signature tune is running. "That's all we have. Until tomorrow, good morning." The red light goes off.

Gay Byrne in action in the studio. Photograph: Kate Horgan.

GAY BYRNE, BROADCASTER

Advice from the Expert

After 35 years in broadcasting, and nearly 25 years with the longest running morning radio show, Gay Byrne still gives the same advice to people wanting to become radio presenters: "Get in as much experience appearing in public as you possibly can. Do anything that involves speaking and performing in public, it is the greatest experience you can have for a broadcasting career - drama, music, debating society, toastmasters - everything."

"Also, if you can specialise in something, do so. Whether it's gardening, music, some hobby, anything. Bring this to radio, with an idea, and get into radio on that basis. That's how I did it."

"Once you are in, you can then become a regular contributor, and if you are good at it, people will notice you and use you again. And then the day will come when someone says 'we need someone to go down to O'Connell Street' and you'll be there."

"'Be Ready.' That's the old Boy Scouts' slogan and that's what you should be. If you are going to sit around wishing for it to happen, it won't."

"From the word go, we were very popular," Gay Byrne remembers about the origins of his radio programme The Gay Byrne Show.

"The rule was, forget the music, read letters, cards, take phone calls and have people in studio."

Prior to that, the Radio One schedule finished early in the day, it was heavily dominated by music programmes, and news programmes were infrequent and shorter than today.

"Our programme was unique at that time, it had talk on it; it was virgin territory - that slot from ten until one."

"We had a huge correspondence from people, and we were doing what Liveline is now doing - taking calls, hearing people talk."

"Maybe you couldn't do that now. These days, there's pretty well non-stop talk from eight o'clock in the morning, until a quarter to three when Liveline finishes. Possibly there's a danger of overkill," says Gay.

Does he have a person in mind when he is broadcasting, talking to that microphone in the studio?

"No, no one person. I have a large audience in my mind, a gang - a crowd."

Radio has an immediacy that television does not.

For television, "you have to try to get the bodies out here (to the studios), whereas for radio, it's simply a matter of taking a phone call. A phone call doesn't work on television, you have a still picture of someone on a phone, or a graphic, and this doesn't work.

"On radio, people are more inclined to talk to you.

"People will tell you their intimate feelings on radio. Even in studio, once you get their eye and sit across from them, it'll be easier for them to talk to you."

You can't do that with television.

GARETH O'CALLAGHAN, 2FM DJ

From the Garret to Gareth in the Afternoon

Presenter and 2FM DJ Gareth O'Callaghan smiles when he remembers his first radio broadcast.

"I was in a sitting room in Dublin, petrified, with an old piano and an old bureau in the same room. In front of me was a nightclub discotheque system, with a microphone stuck on the end of a brush handle!"

It was the pirate radio station, the garret-like Radio Dublin, and he was still in school.

"I always wanted to be a DJ," he said.

In a record shop in town, someone told him they were looking for a DJ for a pirate radio station and he got part-time hours. After four weeks they offered him a full time job, but he turned it down, and studied to be a priest for two years instead.

When he decided that was not for him, he made a demo tape, sent it to Radio Nova, and joined up. From there, he worked for Radio Caroline, and a range of British stations, including BBC Radio 2, before returning to Dublin, and eventually joining 2FM.

He joined in 1989. "I was knocking on the door for ten years, literally," he said.

Gareth's afternoon programme on 2FM evolved into a zany programme, of sound effects, phone characters and funny voices that quickly succeeded, with a blend of music and chat.

It's gone from 120,000 listeners to 350,000 listeners, in three and a half years, since he took over the 3pm to 5pm afternoon slot.

Before the programme, producer Ian Wilson and himself draw up the running order, selecting the times for the different elements like the calls from listeners, and the regular joke items. There's the room at the top for the sport with John Kenny who stays to banter with Gareth at the top of the hour, and Gareth himself chooses items from the newspapers both at home and abroad for his "It Can't be Serious" section.

Broadcasting Assistant Orla outside the screen takes the calls and puts them up on a computer screen which is mirrored on a screen in front of Gareth, so he's aware who's on the line. Other than that, he's on his own in the studio for the two hours he's on air.

Two questions he is constantly asked are: "How do you get away with it?" referring to his sometimes risqué jokes, and "Are there many people in the studio?" due to the many busy sound effects and voices heard throughout the programme.

"It's the theatre factor, it's the image of a complete zoo, complete irreverence," he said. "It's a performance, even if the weather is bad and you have a hangover, you've got to bring that comedy, that light touch."

Gareth O'Callaghan on air on 2FM.   Photograph: Kate Horgan.

A DAY IN THE LIFE OF...

A SUNDAY AFTERNOON ON THE RADIO WITH SUNDAY SPORT

SUNDAY, 19 FEBRUARY, 1995

1.30pm   Producer Pat O'Donovan is sitting in Studio 10 in the Radio Centre, with a sheet of paper, containing columns of reporters, destinations, and matches. That will be his central guide over the three hours of organised chaos, called "Sunday Sport". The four lines on his telephone, as well as the studio phone, are constantly busy.

Upstairs, presenter Des Cahill is updating his results, reading the Sunday papers.

1.45pm   Final preparations are made. A number of reporters are already in place and have rung in. The sound operator puts the sig tune up, and prepares the first commercial break.

1.55pm   Des arrives in studio. Pat knows he has to fill the first 30 minutes with analyses and interviews: there is nothing live until half past two. He prepares four people to preview the busy day's events: Derry vs Down, racing at Punchestown, golf in South Africa, and the Collingwood Cup in UCD.

Micheál O'Muircheartaigh comes through from the Outside Broadcast in Derry; he'll be giving a live commentary later on. Pat passes on information about the state of the pitch and the weather to Des Cahill.

2.00pm   The "This Week" programme is a minute over its time. Pat tells Des to go to Billy George of the *Cork Examiner* first, on the Cork City vs Derry city match. The sig tune rolls. Des checks the results on the computer screen in his studio. Pat checks that the South Africa line is okay. It's the return of the Football League today; it's going to be busy.

Des conducts short interviews on a range of topics, as Pat keeps two calls ahead.

2.20pm   Pat has exhausted his previews, and just in time, he finds Tom Rooney in Portlaoise to talk about the preparations for the match there. Then he has Micheál O'Muircheartaigh ready with his commentary.

2.25pm   Sean O' Ceallacháin fails to come through as Des interrupts Micheál; instead he calls a commercial break. Pascal Mooney rings through to preview Leitrim vs Cork. Pat can hear the national anthem playing in Derry; he cannot interrupt that; Brian Carthy talks about a rainless Dublin vs Kildare preparation.

2.35pm As Micheál O'Muircheartaigh is in full flight on the commentary, he quickly hands back on instruction from Pat to allow Tom Rooney to give details of the first score in Portlaoise, Laois vs Donegal. The aim is to get the scores on air as quickly as they happen from as many venues as possible.

2.40pm Results are coming in from all around. Des takes them on air as quickly as he can, and then returns to Micheál's commentary, all the time watching sports coverage on the TV in the studio, and keeping an eye on the computer screen for results. Across the corridor from the studio, manned phones are also receiving results from a host of stringers around the country.

3.00pm Half time scores are pouring in; Pat lines up reporters to do 30 seconds on air with Des, giving a quick synopsis of their match. Pat keeps a constant eye on the clock over the control desk.

3.25pm Having taken the first race from Punchestown, and bringing in the rest of the half times, Pat makes space for the latest on the South African PGA, and Micheál O'Muircheartaigh continues his commentary.

4.00pm Pat takes a series of reports from games around the country, all the while watching for an opportunity to take a commercial break. Des interviews a player from the Dunloy team who've scored against Athenry, and goes to reporter Brian Carthy live as the team scores. The phone keeps flashing on all lines.

4.11pm Pat fits in the commercial break, and he's getting anxious as the final hour of the programme slips away. Des talks to Peter Smith on the Manchester United vs Leeds Utd match and he gives more results from the English soccer games. Con Murphy comes through from Gortakeegan: suddenly there's an equaliser in the Monaghan Utd. vs Bohemians match. A few minutes later, he's back on the line: there's another goal to talk about.

4.20pm Pat calls another commercial break, and there's a short lull while Gabriel Egan gives a commentary from the RDS Outside Broadcast on the Shamrock Rovers vs Sligo Rovers game.

4.40pm It's time to get in as many results as possible. "The two hurling matches were crackers. It was a busy day," says Pat.

4.58pm He gets Peter Smith on just before the end; he can't get Des Scahill from Punchestown, he gives the racing results to Des to read out instead.

5.10pm Des gets in as many GAA results as possible before the end.

"And we'll be back at 23 minutes to seven this evening with a full results programme. Join me then."

7 A LICENCE TO PRINT MONEY?

Independent and Community Radio

When the legislation to establish independent commercial radio was being debated in Dail Eireann, one deputy commented that getting a licence to broadcast equated to "a licence to print money".

The reality has been somewhat different.

After years of controversy and political wrangling, as well as grossly overstated estimates of its value and its potential, the legislation necessary to legalise independent commercial radio in Ireland was finally passed by Communications Minister Ray Burke in 1987.

At the time, no one could have predicted the level of upheaval which was to occur before the industry settled down and took some shape.

The first two years of the operation of independent radio was marked by change, amalgamation and consolidation.

Probably the most significant casualty was the national station, Century Radio. An opening in a blaze of publicity promised much, but failed to deliver. Within a matter of months it was obvious that Century had problems. Having failed to attract "big names" from RTE, listenership figures didn't reach those needed to attract advertisers in necessary numbers. Transmission difficulties, which resulted in a patchy coverage for its signal, also undermined confidence in the new station. Cut-backs inevitably followed and industrial relations problems were just a symptom of the strain felt by the staff.

The closure of Century was almost inevitable, but the IRTC remains confident that there is room for a second national radio station. Its optimism is not widely shared.

With the national station showing signs of suffering in some areas from competition from local stations, it would be the adventurous investor who would venture down the same road travelled by Century.

But there have been some notable successes in the independent commercial sector, the most obvious being Classic Hits 98FM which from the day it began broadcasting, has commanded a strong listenership and the confidence of advertisers.

Five years on, 21 stations are operating around the country. Since the outset there have been changes in Cork where an original three stations (two in the county, one in the city) have merged to form 96FM which serves both city and county.

In Wicklow two original franchises have merged to form one.

A number of stations have also undergone rationalisation and changes in structure as they have found their place in their own area. In more recent times Shannonside and Northern Sound have entered a co-operation arrangement, and now share a common administration.

The most successful local radio stations operating, in terms of listenership, are those located furthest from the capital.

Highland Radio in Donegal, Radio Kerry, the independent Cork stations and Clare FM are the success stories of local radio.

The situation in Dublin is different with two music stations operating a classic hits formula but making no effort to provide a local radio service. This is radio at its most commercial.

The Independent Radio and Television Commission, (IRTC) the government-appointed body charged with responsibility for regulating the industry, has begun to grant licences to community radio groups across the country. In Dublin the Commission is conscious of the absence of community radio and is granting licences to genuine community groups.

But these are amateur, voluntary groups and the licence will only allow for very localised broadcasting. The very rooted, locally-based broadcasting which has developed outside of Dublin will probably never be available to listeners in the capital.

The Commission has also awarded licences to special interest groups.

Anna Livia FM commenced operations in November 1992, broadcasting community and special interest programmes, in a mainly talk-based format, to the Dublin area. Financed through sponsorship and other voluntary fund-raising activities, its programme content is generated by approximately 300 volunteers.

Late in 1992 an Irish language broadcasting franchise was awarded to Raidió na Life which commenced broadcasting in 1993 to Dublin city and county.

The IRTC also awards a number of temporary licences for special events such as the Galway Arts Festival, and a number of permanent low power licences such as to Beaumont Hospital, in Dublin.

LOCAL RADIO AS COMMUNITY RADIO

Under the legislation governing the industry, the IRTC demands a 20 per cent news/current affairs content, but in practice most of the non-urban stations have no problem achieving this. Local news and local views is what their audience wants and it's what they get.

This is not the case in Dublin however. Here the independent stations 98FM and FM104 depend for their commercial success not on local news and views, but on a diet of "classic hits", music with a minimum of talk. Whereas the non-urban stations concentrate their talk shows in the morning, both of the Dublin commercial stations confine them to late-night listeners. For that, however, FM104's Chris Barry show has developed a successful late night chat show with issues of the day being aired.

AUDIENCE

Listenership figures show that on a national average, the independent stations command a market share of about 43%. When this is analysed on a regional basis, the higher listenership tends to be in areas furthest from Dublin.

Thus Highland Radio in Donegal is one of the most listened to local radio stations, as is Radio Kerry. Nearer to Dublin LMFM is competing in a cluttered environment as is East Coast Radio based in Bray.

NEWS

The demise of Century Radio left a lacuna in the provision of an alternative and independent radio news service. Originally it was filled by 98FM who formed an independent service - Independent Radio News - but in recent times FM104 has also offered a service to local stations: Network Radio News.

Neither service is entirely satisfactory to local stations, since the treatment of stories by 98FM and FM104 can often be unsuitable to the different styles of broadcasting, and the different audience of local independent stations.

The IRTC is currently examining the possibility of regenerating a national alternative station, which would also provide a national news service to independent stations.

Local stations relay broadcasts from the Dublin service and at several points during the day, follow it with their own local news.

Sources of news in independent radio are almost identical to those used by the provincial press: gardai, courts, local political sources, and national news with a local angle.

Sport is a major source of news, talk and coverage on local radio. At weekends, audiences soar as local stations follow closely the exploits of the local team, both at home and away.

Indeed there is no doubt that this is where local radio shines, providing a news and information service which the national station is unable to match.

Nor has independent radio posed any threat to the provincial newspaper industry. It would certainly appear that local radio had simply become an additional, rather than a replacement, source of information.

It is the national network which has most to lose from the the rise of independent radio. In some areas, particularly regions distant from Dublin, the national station is effectively being supplanted by local voices, local news, local information.

LISTENERSHIP FIGURES FOR LOCAL RADIO STATIONS

(JNLR/MRBI Survey – January-December 1994)

North West Radio	66%	WLR FM	46%
Highland Radio	64%	Clare FM	46%
Radio Limerick	62%	Galway Bay FM	43%
Radio Kerry	56%	Shannonside/Northern Sound	40%
Mid West Radio	55%	Tipp FM	39%
South East Radio	52%	LM FM	33%
Cork 96FM/County Sound	50%	Classic Hits 98FM	29%
Radio Kilkenny	49%	East Coast Radio	22%
CKR FM	47%	Radio 3	21%
Tipperary Mid-West Radio	47%	FM 104	20%

LMFM RADIO

Morning Time is Radio Time

LMFM (Louth Meath FM) went on air on September 3rd 1989.

It has had its teething troubles. Station manager Michael Crawley says that an over-emphasis on programming to the detriment of sales and advertising meant that for the first two and a half years LMFM incurred continual losses.

"Getting our sales act together," as Michael Crawley puts it, has meant that more investment can be put into programming and providing a solid local news and information service for listeners.

Now, after five years on air, LMFM is firmly established in the hearts and minds of its audience, commanding about one-third of the market share in its own area.

Thirty people are employed full-time - this includes three full-time news journalists, two full-time sports journalists and a full-time agrijournalist.

"Fifty per cent of the population is rural in our area," says Michael Crawley. "It's the biggest industry."

Sport is big also. Large audiences are commanded at the weekends with a strong emphasis on extensive coverage of local teams - at home and away. This is where local radio shines. National radio cannot provide back-to-back commentary of a county final - but LMFM can.

LMFM's market share is lower than the national average for independent local stations, but as Michael Crawley points out, this is due to intense competition in the area, particularly in the under 35 age group - "the switchers" as he calls them.

LMFM operates in one of the most crowded radio areas in the country. Listeners have access to Dublin music stations 98FM and FM104, both of which reach into this area, as well as Radio One and 2FM, and Downtown Radio from north of the border.

"What makes us different from the rest is our ability to provide local news and information, so we must invest in that side of the operation, even though it is expensive. But it's what gives us an advantage and an audience."

That audience is concentrated in the over 35 age group and is fed a diet heavy on information, particularly news, sport and farming.

Like many other local stations, LMFM is a strong talk radio station - particularly in the morning. This is when the listenership figures are highest. From the time the station opens at 6.30 a.m., up to lunchtime, when the afternoon music show starts, the emphasis is very much on news, information and talk.

It is in programmes such as these that the local community gets to talk to itself. Issues raised vary

LMFM's busy front office in Drogheda.   Photograph: Courtesy of IRTC.

from the state of the local roads to the IRA ceasefire. LMFM's programme co-ordinator Kieran Kissane says much of the programming is audience-driven, but as the producer of the morning chat show "Loose Talk", he feels he also has a responsibility to raise issues which many listeners would not raise on their own initiative.

LMFM takes news bulletins during the day from National Network News provided by FM104 in Dublin. News Editor Barry Daly says the service is not 100 per cent satisfactory. The treatment of a story by a Dublin-based station might not always be the best for a non-Dublin audience.

LMFM runs a strong local news service staffed mostly by young journalists. Ironically one of the biggest problems is keeping them. Michael Crawley ruefully comments that in effect his station is a training ground not only for RTE but for the BBC as well. LMFM trains them and other stations take them.

The LMFM newsroom is similar to any provincial paper. News sources are the same - courts, gardai, the county council and the UDC and local politicians. Sport and agribusiness are also major news items.

With urban centres like Dundalk, Drogheda and Navan, and the proximity of the Border on the one side and north county Dublin on the other, local news is rarely thin in the LMFM newsroom.

News starts at 7.30 a.m. The Eight and Nine bulletins are among the biggest of the day. At lunchtime 30 minutes of mostly local news is transmitted in bulletin form with a presenter lead-in and edited interview soundbites in cart form. Live interviews are rare - except at election time or in the event of a major news story breaking.

Four sports bulletins are broadcast a day and Farm News also features strongly.

Bereavement notices are broadcast after the lunchtime and evening news bulletins. They are notable for the formal tones in which they are delivered by the presenter, but it's the one felt to be the most appropriate.

Other features of this station, marking its local dimension, are the Trading Post (a Buy and Sell slot), Bingo, a Community Events Notice Board and a Community programming hour five nights a week.

Minority music tastes are catered for - after tea. Traditional music and Jazz, Country and Irish and Rock are among the tastes catered for in the programming schedule.

LMFM is a very typical local radio station, following a formula which has become successful right across the country, a formula based on local news and information, and easy listening.

But operating in a crowded environment, it is unlikely to hugely increase its market share in the years to come. Hardly a licence to print money, but nonetheless a successful commercial enterprise.

SUE NUNN, PRESENTER

Talk Driven

Corkwoman Sue Nunn started with Radio Kilkenny a week or so after the station went on air in October 1989. In those days she hosted a Saturday morning two-hour long programme. This was her first experience of radio.

"I was in it about a year before I realised it was for me. My mother had been a journalist and I had spent my childhood traipsing around with her - up and down Patrick Street in Cork, going up the sides of mountains to ICA halls. She was the Women's Editor of the *Cork Examiner* at a time when very few women were journalists.

"I realised then I knew the business - how to get along with people, how to get the stories out of people."

But when she started, as a volunteer, on Kilkenny Radio, she was a complete amateur. Her only qualification, apart from being a mother of three children, was a course in radio journalism in Waterford which included a work experience programme with the BBC in Belfast.

Five years later, Sue Nunn hosts one of independent radio's most successful talk shows on Kilkenny Radio, five days a week, from 12.00 noon to 1.00 and from 1.30 to 2.30. From being a complete amateur on the radio, Sue Nunn is now a consummate professional.

For the vast majority of the time, she is her own producer and researcher, operating entirely on her own. But this is not unusual in local radio. She lines up discs, shoots ads on carts, takes in news bang on time, and conducts interviews live on air, either over the phone or live in studio, and still comes across easy and relaxed to her audience.

Her show, one of the most listened to on the local radio airwaves, is talk driven, a mix of news and information dealt with in an easy style, more like a chat over the kitchen table than a confrontation over a live issue.

In today's issue however a confrontation might be expected. A travellers' encampment in New Ross, just across the county border into Wexford, has been attacked by a group of men wearing balaclavas, vigilante style.

Armed with only a few facts, Sue lines up a call with a woman working in the Travellers' Resource Centre in New Ross.

It's not a new story on these airwaves. The issue has been aired before, in discussions on halting sites, resistance to travellers and the failure of local politicians to deal with the issue satisfactorily.

Radio Kilkenny presenter and reporter Sue Nunn.   Photograph: Courtesy of IRTC.

A local solicitor comes in to discuss a recently published piece of legislation to reform the courts system. The item, although serious, is nevertheless marked by the easy, relaxed style of the presenter.

There's a half hour break for local and national news, giving a breather and time for tea and a sandwich in the staff canteen.

Garda Watch, after lunch, where local gardai come into studio, is no different in style. Even the relatively stiff delivery of the two Gardai doesn't prevent Sue generating the feeling that this is more of a chat.

Before ending, Sue manages to fit in a doctor in studio talking about alcoholism in the context of Drugs Awareness week, and the help that's available for those with drink problems, and their families. And a commentary from a horse race in Gowran Park in also broadcast.

Kilkenny Radio is totally commercial, but has its roots in community radio - and it shows.

Sue Nunn herself is entirely committed to the notion of community input - and doesn't see any conflict between this and the need to be commercially successful.

"I do feel that radio should generate a sense of the community talking to itself on the airwaves, yes.

"But any media organisation has a healthy tension between sales and programming. Because it's so small, the good of the station is important to everyone. But I don't see a conflict between good local radio and being commercially successful.

"I know if we are dealing with the important issues, if we are taking people on, if we are not shying away from the issues, if we are giving people the recognition they need in the community, a proper news service, that is what people want to listen to.

"This shows in the listenership figures and this sells the ads.

"I don't see what we could produce better which would be more commercial. Because what's commercial is what sells and what sells is good radio and good local radio does all these things.

"Good local radio is also highly commercial.

"At a local level radio has got to be community radio - otherwise people won't listen.

8 CHALLENGE AND CHANGE

RTE Television

When television came to Ireland, on December 31st 1961, it was greeted by a street party in Dublin's O'Connell Street, accompanied by scenes of dancing, singing and general jubilation.

The arrival of television was seen as part of the emergence of the modern Ireland. The fact that the state had its own television station was a mark of growing independence and confidence.

Initially, broadcasting hours were limited. The first RTE Authority, established under the 1960 Broadcasting Authority Act, was responsible for one television service and about 43 hours of broadcasting per week, or 2,000 hours in the first year. 45% of this was home produced.

News was the first department to leave Henry Street (RTE's original headquarters). In December 1961 it was transferred "en bloc" to the new building at Montrose, and the first broadcast from the new headquarters was a sound news broadcast. The 1.30 p.m. news was read by Denis Meehan from the new studio on Sunday December 10th 1961. Television had not yet begun.

In 1995 transmission hours by RTE television - on two channels -is estimated at 10,420, of which 2,430 are produced in-house, while 890 hours are sports programmes and 300 produced by independents.

Transmission time now averages 166 hours weekly. Almost half of the output is home produced.

The total budget for television programmes in 1995 is just under sixty million pounds

Television in Ireland is still monopolised by RTE, a semi-state company run by an Authority appointed by the government of the day and a Director General chosen from a panel supplied to the Minister responsible for Broadcasting.

With a staff of almost 2,000 and an income in 1993 of 130 million pounds, RTE is one of the country's largest and most successful companies.

RTE's two channels broadcast to seven out of 10 Irish adults on an average day.

RTE television is also responsible for two orchestras - the National Symphony Orchestra and the RTE concert Orchestra.

Television is the largest part of the organisation, responsible for the greatest number of transmission hours, largest number of staff and biggest budget.

The Television Programmes division is responsible for areas as diverse as Sports, Current Affairs, Young People's Programmes, Agricultural Programmes, Religious Programmes, Features and Variety.

Significantly, the Independent Productions Unit operates under the auspices of the Television Programmes Division.

And of course RTE television has undertaken the staging and production of three Eurovisions in a row, probably the biggest ventures ever undertaken by RTE.

Among the programmes produced by this division are the Late Late Show and Kenny Live, both products of TV Variety.

Checkup and Head to Toe are products of the Features section.

Tuesday File, Marketplace, Questions and Answers and Prime Time as well as the more recent addition Farrell, are all from the Current Affairs stable. Election and budget coverage and special events are also undertaken by current affairs.

Sports programming is a significant part of television programmes - especially during set piece events like the World Cup or the Olympics.

The relationship between RTE and the Government has had its uneasy moments over the years, among

them the sacking of the Authority following the broadcasting of an interview with a member of the IRA - before the enactment of Section 31 of the Broadcasting Act in the early 1970s.

The possibility of an independent third channel remains still just that - a possibility, following the controversy between the IRTC and TV3 about the licence for an independent channel.

But the close relationship between RTE television and its audience has remained a feature of RTE television over the years. Despite considerable opposition from British and satellite channels, RTE still produces programmes attracting the highest audiences.

INTERVIEW

LIAM MILLER, RTE

Change on the Horizon

Liam Miller is Director of Television Programmes in RTE. This is the biggest division in the organisation, responsible for over 10,000 transmission hours every year and a budget of nearly sixty million pounds.

Liam Miller is in no doubt that television in Ireland stands at a pivot of change.

"I think we are probably at an important point historically both in terms of the politics and culture of the island, and in terms of a whole range of initiatives in broadcasting," says Miller.

"Not least among these initiatives is the 1993 Broadcasting Act which dealt primarily with production, but we now have a Green Paper which specifically addresses broadcasting."

Miller is in no doubt that the 1993 Act, with its requirement on RTE to make a significant investment in independent productions, is having an impact – both internally and externally.

"By the time the Act takes full effect it will be beyond the limit of the organisation to simply restructure its expenditure to cope with the demands placed on it by the legislation. When we reach the 20 per cent, we in RTE will have to look at a redistribution of the way we produce for television," he said.

"In a situation where at least one in every four programmes produced in Ireland is produced by an independent, there are obvious implications for the schedule, and for the way we structure our own broadcasting resources. There are also implications for the way broadcasting is funded."

"Based on the present funding structure, it would be difficult to achieve the transfers (the Act requires 20 per cent transfer of RTE's programme budget to go to independents by 1999) while leaving RTE's own production structure, which as been the largest single national production asset in the audio–visual sector, intact."

But Miller is in no doubt that by then, the independent sector will be able to stand on its own two feet.

"If it were up and running in 1999 I can't see any circumstances in which it would not survive. What is going to happen over the next two or three years, is the development of companies which are genuine TV suppliers.

"At the moment they need to cover a number of bases, because the industry isn't big enough, but by the end of the few years you will have viable independent producers."

Miller reminds us that even before the legislation required RTE to support the independent sector, the national broadcaster spent £4m on independent Irish productions, principally entertainment and documentaries.

Eurovision

Miller denies that the Eurovision Song Contest has dominated the programme division over the last number of years.

"The reality is that in each of the three years when we have produced Eurovision, we have not reduced the number of hours of television produced in the preceding years.

"You do pluck people out who have particular skills you need, and tie them up in the Eurovision. For programme people this can be for six or seven months, less for technical people, and naturally this does have an effect elsewhere.

"But from the first win in Malmo, we have been determined that Eurovision does not distract us from our normal production. We have in fact increased drama output, lengthened our autumn–winter schedule of feature programmes – this means more Checkup and Family Matters, for instance – and this has all been done since Malmo."

Current Affairs

Current Affairs is always a talking point in the schedule. In recent years the replacement of Today Tonight with a different approach of reducing the amount of time given to in-studio analysis of issues of the week – or day – has resulted in criticism that the section is unable to respond quickly to big stories.

Miller defends the change – but signals that a review might be on the way.

"In April 1992 we were in a situation where Today Tonight had been on the air for 13 seasons. This had been RTE's longest current affairs series. The Today Tonight format had evolved at a time when the news gathering technology was a film-based one and the constraints of the technology dictated that news and current affairs responded differently and played different roles in the schedule.

"The reality now is that with the adoption of new technologies, and especially with the increased investment in news, the balance of supplying information has changed considerably.

"The changed state of politics was the other factor. A period of relative political stability means that a format of three or four nights of studio-based analysis was not justified, or suitable and was simply difficult to sustain.

"The political dynamic has also changed and one of the essential elements of programming is going back on a regular basis and asking is this the best way of providing the service, taking on board the political landscape, programming developments and so on. So, yes, change in this section is definitely possible."

A merger with the news division is not one of them – at least not at the moment.

But change is certainly on the horizon.

Transmission hours are being looked at, and an earlier start is likely.

"There is a developing audience for morning television in this country. The Atlanta Olympics might provide an opportunity to experiment with an earlier starting time.

"I also believe there is an audience for late night television. Our recent initiative "The End" had demonstrated a demand for late night broadcasting at the weekend but I suspect it is there for seven nights of the week."

Drama

"In the immediate short term we have sought and got financial and corporate support for an expansion in our drama output. The Authority is committed to spending over three and a half million in this area over the next three years, over and above normal spending, including co-productions. The priority would be for short series or one-offs."

"As part of that, we will be looking again at Fair City and Glenroe – at the story lines, their relevance. And we will also be looking at greater frequency, or at at least one of the two becoming a year-round possibility."

MARY RAFTERY, PRODUCER

Like Conducting an Orchestra

More than ten years later, Mary Raftery clearly remembers her first assignment as a Producer.

"There was a six month training course – three months of learning the job, and three months placement. I was assigned to what was then Landmark, the agricultural programme, and the first item I worked on as a Producer was on early fat lamb," she remembers with a laugh.

Mary Raftery came to RTE via investigative journalism. She had previously worked on *In Dublin*, *Magill* and the *Sunday Tribune* as one of an ad hoc group of journalists whose hard hitting incisive writing has not been matched since.

She applied to RTE as a Producer/Director on the basis of a public advertisement. "I didn't know anybody in RTE."

But she readily admits the route she took is only one example.

"I have worked on current affairs and on information-type programmes, but there are producer/directors who work on music, drama, light entertainment – nothing to do with journalism.

"The role of the producer is to be the leader of the team – not in the sense of handing out the work, but in the sense of facilitating the creative abilities of all the members of the team and using them to the best effect. The analogy of Conductor of an Orchestra is a good one – the orchestra is only as good as the conductor, but without the orchestra, the conductor is nothing."

At different times the producer/director can find him or herself in different roles. The director part of the job, for instance, can be to be the captain of the studio ship with a live programme on air, co-ordinating everything and making sure it happens.

As Series Producer on Checkup, all of Mary's organisational and planning skills come into play. The team operates a three-week system – one week filming, one week viewing, deciding and editing, another week editing and planning ahead.

"You can't do enough planning ahead," she says.

And it's a highly creative role.

"While we're not operating on a completely blank sheet here, from the point of view that we are reconstructing people's experiences and describing medical procedures, there is a high level of creativity involved in visualising the story, making it happen on television," she says.

PAT KENNY, TELEVISION PRESENTER

Broadcaster Pat Kenny started his TV career in children's programmes. "The programme was called Babaro - I wrote scripts and songs for it."

It's a long way from interviewing politicians and the public on his morning radio programme five days a week, or talking to Garth Brooks on "Kenny Live" on a Saturday night, but Pat believes this introduction to the medium of broadcasting was invaluable.

"It was an easy way to learn television techniques, to see how the VTR machine worked, what the floor manager did, and the discipline on the floor of the studio. All that is absolutely vital to understand - the function of each and every constituent process that makes up a programme.

"Many people don't realise how complicated a television programme is, especially a live programme," he said. "On Kenny Live, for example, you could be de-rigging a band in one corner of the set, while conducting a personal interview on the other.

"For some reason, people tend to be more verbose on television than radio, maybe because they feel more exposed. But it's harder to conduct a short, sharp interview on television than radio."

And it's complicated by the numbers of people and the amount of equipment.

There are four cameras in studio, possibly a cable person to ensure the camera's cables don't get tangled, four sound operators controlling the microphones, there's the autocue operator, the designer, and the researchers are probably floating around as well. The floor manager is watching everything - he's the eyes and ears of the director who's up in the control box. There's the vision mixer changing the shots seen on screen, and behind the scenes, there's the make-up people - all of these contribute as part of the team to the final product.

"I find studio audiences who've never been on a live programme before are amazed by how many people there are, and how quickly it's all done," said Pat.

He believes there are three separate, but simultaneous levels, to being a television presenter.

"Firstly there's the direct interview, listening and talking to the interviewee."

"On the second level, you have to monitor how the interview is going - am I getting what I want, for example? And thirdly, there are the decisions to be made about the shape of the show; for example, if one item runs a few minutes over, you have to make mental calculations to save that time later."

He's done Kenny Live for seven years now; before that he's remembered as a presenter in Television Current

"In the hot seat." TV Presenter Pat Kenny.   Photograph: Kate Horgan.

Affairs, on Today Tonight, and Public Account, as well as election coverage.

There's the memorable occasion when the central computer predicting the results broke down.

"It requires a lot of confidence to be able to handle that situation. I remember noticing that Brian Lenihan's name didn't appear on the list for Dublin West, and that Rory O'Hanlon had also vanished. We put such faith in technology, and it took the team too long to accept that something was breaking down; what was happening was that as soon as someone was elected, the computer rejected them."

"I got tremendous adrenalin, a great buzz from that. It's one of my favourite memories. It was down to me, I had to depend on my own wits to get it right, and I did."

Pat rarely gets nervous before a programme. "I'm just one of those people who doesn't seem to get nervous, I might get a bit edgy just before the off, especially if it's a new series. That's something a lot of people in television have in common - they don't get an attack of the nerves."

Like many successful broadcasters, Pat had never planned to have a career in radio or television.

"It was a complete accident, not planned at all. I had been teaching Chemical Engineering in Bolton Street for two years, and I was a bit bored. I saw the ad. and applied for a job as part-time radio announcer in RTE radio. At first it was part-time, and then I worked full-time during the long summer holidays, and then I moved from full-time to part-time teaching, and eventually I came in full time. There was no such thing as Communications courses then."

The announcer job was an apprenticeship, and he went from there through a variety of jobs in RTE, learning new skills all the time; these included stints in Radio One and 2FM, in television Business and Current Affairs programmes, and then into Light Entertainment and Kenny Live. And not forgetting the children's programmes, of course.

And what next for the man who had done so much?

"Who knows? Wait and see."

ANYTHING HAPPENING?

THE RTE NEWSROOM

With 120 full-time journalists and another 80 or so management, production and administration staff, the RTE newsroom buzzes with activity all day long.

Around 6.30a.m. the overnight staff, the 2FM newsreader and the Radio One overnight sub editor, will end their shift and be replaced by the early staff on the Radio One desk, as well as the 2FM desk. A reporter assigned to Radio One will start his/her shift at this time, beginning by making a series of check calls to garda stations, fire brigades and coastal rescue.

They are joined by to the Morning Ireland presenters and programme editor as they pick up where the night-time team has left off. They will discuss the prepared items, and divide them up between them. The newspapers are checked for overnight developments.

Around 7a.m. the journalist doing "It says in the Papers" starts.

A little later the Senior Foreign Editor, the News Editor and the Editor of the lunchtime TV news are joined by the Programme Editor of the News at One (radio) to discuss the morning news list, both domestic and foreign. This marks the beginning of the process of preparing the lunchtime programmes.

Foreign news is an important part of the daily newslist. With a sparse coverage of foreign correspondents, RTE relies heavily on its membership of the European Broadcasting Union, which supplies pictures to members, several times a day, from the world's hotspots. These pictures are then used by RTE reporters to tell the story. A big story in Ireland, such as a meeting of prime ministers, foreign ministers or heads of state, will be offered by RTE to other members of the EBU.

By the time reporters start appearing, from 8.30 a.m. onwards, a list of assignments has been prepared for them. They are matched with crews for television and dispatched on their stories, equipped with a mobile phone.

A television sub editor is responsible for the "heads"– the headlines on television both morning and afternoon, transmitted from the Newsroom itself.

For the rest of the day, each desk will have its own team preparing for the next programme or bulletin. As Morning Ireland finishes, the News at One and lunchtime television news is gearing up. The 2FM desk hums constantly, turning out bulletins on the hour. Similarly the Radio One desk doesn't let up.

On the television desk, the News Editor is joined by an assistant, who will act as a linchpin between reporters, correspondents and crews, as well as keeping abreast of ongoing developments. She or he will stay there until the

Nine O'Clock news is off the air. Conferences at regular intervals during the day discuss stories as they develop and decide the technical back up needed. Will there be a live interview on location?

Reporters and correspondents phone in regularly, updating their stories. The computer system allows all users, including those abroad and in the regions, access to material as soon as it is filed.

Walking into the newsroom structure the Nuacht desk, a team at once separate, but an integral part of, the Newsroom structure.

By mid afternoon the interlinking wheels in the machine are all working at full speed. The biggest programme of the day, the Six One bulletin, demands a lot of attention, and gets it. By the time it is getting into top gear, the first of the evening reporters on the Morning Ireland shift is arriving for work.

After six, the atmosphere is quieter and by the time Network News goes on the air, the Newsroom is almost deserted. By midnight or 1 a.m. the Morning Ireland reporters are heading for home.

Then it's over to the overnight person on the 2FM desk, and on the Radio One desk, to keep the show on the road until the next morning comes around again.

JOE MULHOLLAND, DIRECTOR OF NEWS, RTE

Directing for the Future

As it approaches the end of the century, the RTE newsroom is facing up to the challenge of competition presented by the availability to its audience of round-the-clock and often live coverage of major news events. To meet it, RTE news has increased its output and moved towards more live coverage of the big stories of the day. Developments in editing technology is changing the role of the broadcast journalist in both radio and television, while RTE's programmes are now available to a wider audience than ever, due to transmission by satellite.

Since Joe Mulholland became Director of News in RTE, output has increased significantly. There are now more news bulletins on RTE television than ever before.

"This has to do with competition", says Mulholland by way of explanation.

The competition is coming from BBC and ITN and more recently from Sky which can provide rolling, non-stop, live news from the scene of a breaking and ongoing news story.

"We can't have rolling news except on the big occasions", says Mulholland. "But we have had to follow the competition by having more news bulletins and more updates. As a result we have bulletins on television from 10.00 a.m., we have the One o clock, the Six One has expanded and the Nine has been developed in a particular way."

"For the moment we have reached the limit of our resources on television, but on the radio side we are planning to develop a late night news programme. We have to match people's changing patterns of behaviour in the supply of news".

The future is certainly in live news and the number of live inserts into bulletins has increased. This has been helped by changing technology.

"We have more and more capacity for live television, especially from outside Dublin. What we are planning is a permanent satellite on a transponder which would enable us to have live SNG - Satellite News Gathering, feeding live into bulletins".

RTE news has a strong commitment to the regions, reflecting the station's public service mandate. An experiment in July 1994 in Regional Television, which was to have been a precursor for regular regional television, proved problematic.

"The footprints of our transmitters were not accurate, having been adjusted over the years. This meant that some regions got output destined for other communities. So we have had to put the idea into cold storage for the moment. However there is no doubt that there is a future for regional television. It is necessary and it will happen".

RTE reporters have done more travelling in the last few years than ever before. Some of this results from the Newsroom's dedication to covering President Robinson's trips abroad, but it also comes from Mulholland's commitment to have an Irish voice reporting the world's big stories.

"We cannot just sit back and have other people's versions of these events as the only one broadcast. We are a sovereign state and it is not good enough any more, with a world becoming smaller by the day and with people travelling that world, to simply accept someone else's version of events."

In that context Mulholland points to what he calls the "lacuna" of the absence of a correspondent in the United States, although the possibility of sending reporters regularly, rather than basing a correspondent there full time, is probably more real.

Mulholland constantly looks ahead, and sees developments in technology as significantly changing the way the newsroom works.

Specifically he points to self-editing, in both radio and television, as important in the ever changing role of the journalist and their ability to control their material.

But what is the biggest challenge ahead?

"I would say that we need to retain the authoritative, credible voice of the country, to which people will turn when they want to be informed. Therefore we need to maintain the standard of broadcasting and journalism that we have always had. Resources, technology, improving our production - all this is important is we are to keep and maintain our position."

A NIGHT IN THE LIFE OF...

THE NINE O'CLOCK NEWS

WEDNESDAY, 23 NOVEMBER 1994

It was an average day in the life of the Nine O'Clock news. Although it will be remembered as falling only a week after Dick Spring had declared his intention of resigning from the Partnership Government with Fianna Fail, this day did not yield a momentous story. Nevertheless the ongoing political crisis remained at the top of the newslist.

Preparation for the bulletin begins in mid afternoon when the preliminary conference, or meeting, of the main players in the programme team, takes place. It happens in a tiny, box-like room which forms part of the newsroom proper and barely fits the number of people attending. Some are standing.

The programme editor, Ed Mulhall, the chief sub editors of the day, Don McManus and Conor Quinn, as well as the presenter, Brian Dobson, accompanied by the production assistants and director of the day, discuss the possible shape of the programme.

By seven o'clock, when the second and final conference takes place, the discussion is more focussed. And it's joined by a member of the News Graphics Department. This is an experienced team. All will be familiar with the stories of the day already, since most staff work on more than one programme. Each has his or her own task to perform and understands their place in the process. There are many other contributors to the programme - reporters, news editors, subeditors, studio staff, technical editing and production staff, but this is the group which gets and keeps the programme on air.

The discussions are short and to the point. It's now only two hours to airtime. Andy Sheppard, Foreign Editor, offers a "full sound clip" of President Clinton speaking about GATT. It's accepted.

Programme Editor Ed Mulhall tells the team that Gareth O'Connor, one of two reporters assigned specifically to the programme, will have a report on haters of the Manchester United football team. This coincides with a Manchester United vs. Gothenburg match. It's a light story - a "kicker" for Part Two of the bulletin.

A running order has been prepared by Don McManus. It's gone through methodically. Everyone needs to be clear on the order of the stories, what reporter is doing them, and what they are about.

This list will be distributed to other staff around the building- in editing, in the room where tapes are transmitted from and to the technical staff in the studio. Any changes made in the meantime means a new running order has to be sent to all these people - much of the "running" is done by casual staff, often students, known as "runners". They also "run" to the library and to editing suites with tapes required by reporters or directors.

Marion from News Graphics discusses the "picture window" for each story - that's the box which appears behind the shoulder of the presenter. Marion asks how she should represent tonight's main story - it's a row between Fianna Fail and Labour over a decision on legislation regarding abortion. It's agreed it's difficult to represent, but finally it is decided to use a picture of the Four Courts since the legislation has resulted from a Supreme Court decision.

Una Claffey rings from Leinster House as the meeting is breaking up - she will have a new piece for nine. She tells Ed Mulhall that the Fianna Fail National Executive is meeting, but feels it's more of a Morning Ireland story. No, she won't need a crew before nine, she says.

With everyone agreed on the ingredients of the programme, the meeting ends. It's now 7.15 p.m. and the team members return to their work stations to be ready for nine o clock. Unless there is a late-breaking story, the process should be a smooth one.

During the next hour or so, all the pieces are put together. The subeditors liaise with the chief sub, making a note of what stories have to be cut or altered. A Teaser and Promo which will run before the ad break in the middle of the programme, are agreed and the sub goes off to cut the necessary clips.

Members of the Foreign Unit write their scripts and head for the Editing suites. Reporters assigned to the Home Desk are sitting near the news desk in case any new story breaks. It's generally a quiet time of the day for them, unless theirs is a changing story. Some go to editing to cut back their 6 o' clock packages.

The news editor has drawn up an early news list for the following morning, based on continuing stories such as the political crisis, and diary items. If necessary she will assign reporters and crews to early markings.

Brian Dobson is reading and in some cases re-writing lead-ins to stories. He will have gone to the Make-Up Department and emerged with a false sun tan. A tube of clear plastic hangs down his back - that's his earpiece. Each presenter has one and it connects to the desk in the studio, allowing for communication with the editor and director, while the bulletin is on air.

Brian also writes headlines for the opening sequence and in some cases discusses stories with reporters in order to get the essential point for the headline.

Tonight he rings Donal Kelly to discuss the political story – the row between Labour and Fianna Fail over who decided what on abortion legislation before the administration broke up.

He finishes the conversation and goes into studio with 2 minutes to spare. In the control room the Director is in charge. Sitting in the centre of the front row, he watches a bank of TV screens in front of him and issues directions to the crew in the studio and to the floor manager who is in the studio with Brian.

Again the crew work as a team. The production assistant counts down each videotape. One minute left. Thirty seconds. Out words are... Ten seconds. Five, four, three, two one.

The bulletin runs smoothly (see Running Order)*, the only hiccup being in Part Two when Sean Whelan's tape can't be found. The problem is identified around ten past nine and several phone calls are made in an effort to find it. In the end the six o' clock version, which is still in the Output Room, is broadcast.

It turns out later that the name on the tape had been changed, but this didn't coincide with the name on the running order - an example of the importance of good communication.

At half nine, a relaxed team leaves the studio, another programme over. Brian Dobson discusses some details with the Programme Editor as they walk back the short distance to the Newsroom. There's always room for improvement, but as bulletins go, this was smooth.

```
23/11/94 21:29 cqu ?:?? !13-9 TV R/O
9 TV R/O            b0 u0 m0 s0    21:29:09                    Display 1
9 TV Running Order                                            23/11/94
         Story Slug    Dur.  Runs  Stat  Filed Intime   Src.
━━━━━━━━━━━━━━━━━━━━━━━━━━━━━━━━━ SEGMENT 1 ━━━━━━━━━━━━━━━━━━━━━━━━━━━━━━
01    9vtOPENING      0:32 00:15  22b 20:59 09:00:00 VT7
                                            09:00:32
02    WIDE SHOT                             09:00:32 LASR
                                            09:00:32
03    9BIRD           0:38 00:37  33d 20:59 09:00:32
04    9vtBIRD         2:25 02:25  33A 19:32 09:01:10 VT
05                                          09:03:35
                                            09:03:35
06    9UNA            0:13 00:13  33D 20:53 09:03:35
                                            09:03:48
Y7    XUNALIVE        1:16 01:16  33A 20:51 09:03:48 DAIL
```

9 O'Clock News Running Order

BRIAN DOBSON, RTE NEWSCASTER

The Face of the Nine O' Clock News

Brian Dobson is only 34, but the authority he asserts on screen seems to belong to someone well beyond those years. His Clark Kent looks and serious tones belie his relaxed approach off-screen, but are well suited to the look of the Nineties newscaster.

In this regard RTE has followed general television trends. While newscasters were once recruited purely from the acting profession, primarily for presentation rather than journalistic skills, these days newscasters are recruited from the ranks of the journalists.

Brian Dobson is a good example of the journalist as presenter, with the ability to conduct a television interview, present a radio programme, or compile a straightforward news report.

Originally from Dublin, Brian Dobson began to study Communications at the College of Commerce in Rathmines, but never finished the course. Instead he found himself working on the then illegal, but very successful Dublin pirate station, Radio Nova. From there, in the early eighties, he moved to Belfast to work with BBC Northern Ireland as a reporter and sometime presenter of their version of Morning Ireland: Good Morning Ulster.

In 1987 he moved back to Dublin to work in RTE, originally as a reporter on "This Week", the Sunday current affairs programme. It was through the development of the fixed business slot on the expanded Six One programme, and through "Marketplace", that Brian Dobson came to television presenting. His presenting of the Nine O' Clock news began in 1991.

"I see the Nine as the definitive digest of the main stories of the day," he says. "We have tended in more recent times to reduce the actual number of stories done, but to cover the big story in a really comprehensive fashion by probably taking more than one bite at it.

"I don't think RTE should go down the tabloid road. I don't think we have to. The Irish audience are interested in serious things, in politics, and while our production has improved considerably and the look of the programme has become more high-tech and showbizzy, I think at the end of the day it's the story that engages the audience and keeps them watching."

Newscaster Brian Dobson behind the scenes.   Photograph: Kate Horgan.

CHARLIE BIRD, SPECIAL CORRESPONDENT

The Messenger on the Plinth

Charlie Bird, Special Correspondent, has worked in television news for fifteen years. In that time he has earned himself an undisputed reputation as Ireland's best known television news reporter.

His fame probably started when he interviewed Fr Niall O'Brien in his prison cell in the Philippines during the eighties, when the Marcos regime was at its most powerful and oppressive.

But for many viewers, it is Charlie Bird's role as confessor to politicians as they emerge from the latest political crisis, that has made him a household name and face.

By now it seems that even the smallest of political crises wouldn't be complete without the sight of Charlie Bird on the plinth outside Leinster House. His characteristically staccato, breathless and overblown style, as well as his almost childlike wonder at the story he is telling, have become an accepted, if entirely unique, part of the journalistic landscape of this country.

Bird himself is obviously proud of the role he has developed for himself.

"Myself and Caroline Erskine started to come down to Leinster House to get politicians' reactions to the events of the day, when we were both on the newsdesk as reporters during the early eighties. That's how it started.

"Before that political coverage was confined to reportage of Dáil debates and reports from the political correspondents from the Dáil studio. But I feel what I am doing has broadened political coverage a lot and given people a much better insight into what's happening in Leinster House."

"The plinth has become a focal point. I spend the day there sometimes. I start around at Government Buildings on Merrion Street and get some reaction from ministers going in. But in general I spend my day here with a camera crew. This is my office.

"And I'm here no matter what the weather. And there have been some very cold days. If it's raining I'll go into the security hut at the entrance gate, but mostly I'm outdoors all the time."

Charlie can recall a number of stories which he was able to "break" by virtue of being the messenger on the plinth. They include the first announcement of moves against party leaders – Haughey, Reynolds, Dukes among them.

But there are rules of operation in this business. The plinth is a rectangular raised granite area in the centre of the yard in front of Leinster House. Reporters are

Charlie Bird surrounded by his equipment: voice, phone and cameras.   Photograph: Kate Horgan.

not supposed to stray off it. Thus if politicians want to avoid the assembled pack, they keep off the plinth.

Getting the story back to Montrose has become a lot simpler than in the past. Usually a courier carries back a tape with raw interviews, voiced links from Bird as well as a "PTC", or "piece to camera", where the reporter speaks directly to camera.

Once the tape reaches the Newsroom, it is taken over by a subeditor, who has discussed its contents with Bird and knows what the end product should look like. Bird will phone in his "lead-in" - the opening to his story read by the presenter.

A "live link" i.e. a broadcast link, is now available outside Leinster House and live interviews now form a regular part of news reporting from the Dáil. When the story is big, such as the political upheaval at the end of 1994, a mobile editing suite is set up in Buswells Hotel to allow for on-the-spot editing.

Like all reporters out in the field, Bird is expected to supply material for both Radio One and the 2FM news services. Thus he phones the Radio One studios and records a "voiced piece" for transmission, with a separate sign-off for each service.

By now "the plinth" has become one of the essential places to be when reporting the political story. When the story is big, the plinth can get very crowded with reporters, photographers and camera crews and some interviews more closely resemble a rugby scrum.

And Charlie Bird will no doubt be near the centre of that scrum, still asking the questions. And when the occasional visitors to the plinth have gone and the story has become a bit more pedestrian, then Charlie Bird will still be sending his stories from the plinth.

9 GOING IT ALONE

Independent Television

The injection of funds resulting from the establishment of RTE's Independent Productions Unit in 1993 has led to a mushrooming in the independent television sector in this country.

The unit, established on foot of legislation requiring RTE to devote eventually up to 20 per cent of its programming budget to independent productions, received 700 submissions for its first full year of operations – and independent productions - 1994.

The number of submissions for the 1995 round was 1,000.

Among the programmes emanating from the independent sector have been Ear to the Ground, Stateside, The Blackboard Jungle, Comely Maidens, Megazone, The Lyrics Board and Rich and Rare Land.

The legislation which resulted in the Unit, the 1993 Broadcasting Authority (Amendment) Act, was responding to years of calls for government help for the independent film and programme-making sector. Taken with the tax reliefs to the film industry, the government's measures have seen the industry take off.

COMMISSIONING

According to Clare Duignan, who heads up the Unit, it aims to provide quality and original programming for the RTE schedules.

The Unit holds an average of three commissioning rounds each year – they are advertised in the national press and in the RTE Guide.

The type of programme sought can change each year, depending on RTE's programme scheduling requirements. In addition to the types of programmes specified in the rounds advertised, the unit is also open to other proposals not specified.

The number of programmes, or series of programmes, commissioned also changes from year to year. In 1994 approximately 271 hours of programming was commissioned.

The number of submissions received varies too, but figures indicate a growing interest. In 1994 almost 700 were received, but in 1995 it had grown to almost 1000.

BUDGET

The annual budget for the IPU is set down by the 1993 legislation, rising each year as follows:

- 1994   5 million pounds
- 1995   6.5 million pounds
- 1996   7.5 million pounds
- 1997   8.5 million pounds
- 1998   10 million pounds

The legislation requires that in each subsequent financial year, either £12.5 million or twenty per cent of television programme expenditure in the preceding financial year, is spent on independent productions.

INFORMATION AND HELP

The unit has published *Guidelines on Commissioning Procedures* – this is available on request. An Information Seminar for the Independent Sector was held in June 1994 and another is planned for 1995.

And Clare Duignan reminds would-be applicants that sponsorship is also welcome – but that independent producers should not approach potential sponsors until the IPU has at least indicated an interest in the project.

DAVID HARVEY, INDEPENDENT PRODUCER

The Brains Behind Crimeline

David Harvey is an independent producer – or a commercial producer, as he prefers to call himself. Commercial he certainly is – he is involved in no less than four companies.

They are all located in mews buildings in the shadow of the Peppercannister Church in Dublin. Sixteen people are employed and he says there is the potential for more. Turnover is about one million pounds annually.

Reelgood studios, incorporating both television and radio recording and editing suites, produces a quarter of all the radio advertisements that go out on air in Ireland.

It is the core business, but mindful of the possibility of sudden market changes, he developed Midas Productions, a television production company.

Midas produces Crimeline, the most successful independent programme on air at the moment – and has the second biggest audience after Glenroe.

Harvey is the brains behind Crimeline.

"There was an amount of luck involved," he says, explaining how it came about.

"I had spent a number of years doing continuity in RTE, so I know Liam Miller, who at the time was Head of Presentation. This was in the late eighties.

"I had a personal family connection with the Garda Commissioner and he was supportive of the idea for the programme.

"When I approached Liam Miller, now Director of Television, with the idea, he really liked it, but he said – 'I have no money'. This, remember, was in the days before the development of the Independent Productions Unit.

"So I approached Hibernian Insurance and to give them their due, they were prepared to run with the idea, without even seeing a single programme.

"Having Marian (Finucane) up front really helped of course. And it was a hit, a monster hit, from the first night it went out."

The Crimeline team - which includes Harvey himself, Kevin Cantrell the production manager, three or four members of the Gardai, John Caden who is editor and scriptwriter, meets two days after the transmission of the previous programme, to plan ahead for the next one.

Ideas are assessed for their reconstructability, as well as their crime-solving potential.

Scripts are developed and reconstructions are shot –

Independent TV Producer, David Harvey, in his production office.   Photograph: Kate Horgan.

they take a day each. The material is edited in Reelgood and the team then arrives in RTE on the Monday of transmission. From 4 p.m. they rehearse and the programme is transmitted at 9.30.

"It's successful because it's watchable. It looks well, it's strong drama, and people generally know someone who is involved in it."

Crimeline is the Midas flagship, but in the first instance Midas was a corporate video company which developed into making independent productions. Its main business remains in the corporate world. Midas clients include Woodchester, the National Irish Bank, First National, Ericsson, Intel and AST.

Harvey had been operating in the commercial sector before the advent of the 1993 legislation requiring RTE to devote a certain percentage of its television budget to the independent sector. But he recognises that in fact RTE had already begun to develop a policy on the use of independently-produced material.

He instances not only Midas Productions, but also Promedia, which produced "The Motor Show", Windmill Lane, Yellow Asylum, and MD which produced Murphy's Australia, as examples of companies supplying material to RTE.

In the early Eighties Green Apple Productions, the brainchild of the late Vincent Hanley with Conor MacAnally, had produced the very successful MT USA, before satellite television brought us music television.

And, going back further, Harvey instances the Radharc programmes – all independently produced.

Harvey feels that RTE's current, post-legislation approach to independent productions, spreads resources too thinly.

"RTE could call on, and rely on, a small number of the larger production companies to come up with a number of series. Companies such as my own, having been in the marketplace for some time, can come up with the money needed upfront, we know how to finance co-productions."

"Instead, RTE is supporting between 40 and 50 small, in some cases one-person operations and the relationship and approach the organisation has to those operators, and companies like my own, is exactly the same. It doesn't make sense."

Harvey would welcome more competition in the television marketplace.

"Competition would make an enormous difference, simply by supplying a second outlet for independent producers. And I believe it would give RTE a very different focus also."

The industry is growing and Harvey believes the next few years should be good ones for the independent sector.

JOBS AND THE FUTURE

Introduction

"How did you become a journalist?"

It's a common question to many an established writer or broadcaster from a student or aspiring journalist, and a very relevant one.

How people get jobs in newspapers, and in RTE, remains as varied as the people who work in these organisations.

But there are common threads.

Increasingly, newcomers have done a recognised training course giving them the basic skills of the trade.

And they have spent some time getting job experience in the workplace and doing freelance work to get their foot in the door. Until eventually a short term contract comes along, or the person's work gets noticed by senior personnel in the workplace.

And in all cases, there's a lot of hard work, and not a little luck. Being in the right place at the right time is always a help.

In this section, we examine the world of work for the Irish journalist today, from the established greats of broadcasting to the delving political reporter. There's a great variety in media-related jobs too - from the public relations consultant to the political handler.

Freedom of information is a central concern for working journalists, as well as a knowledge of the legal limitations on print and broadcasting. There are serious penalties for journalists who break the laws of libel and slander; many think the Irish laws are too restrictive, and this chapter outlines the changes the Government is proposing in this area.

And also in this section, we examine what the future holds for journalism. As part of the ongoing communications revolution, the working tools of journalism are changing rapidly and radically. Computers and telephone lines are performing tasks never imagined a decade ago, and this section looks at these changes.

And this revolution is causing changes in the world of information storage, too. The vital knowledge of journalists - how to find out more - is contained in libraries and on computer disks, not to mention the dog-eared contact book.

Even with the CD, the laptop, and the satellite, some things will never change, and the handwritten contacts book will remain the central tool of many a future journalist.

10 GETTING THE HEADLINES

Working in the Media

Journalism is a job with huge variety, rewards and not a little stress. It can be difficult, sometimes boring and often challenging. People who become journalists are a bit different.

A job in the media is competitively sought by school leavers, college graduates and people moving from other professions. Many ambitious for the limelight see themselves as the next Brian Dobson or Emily O'Reilly, the next editor of a daily paper, or the local reporter who scoops the big guns.

The media is part of the general services industry and has expanded as a sector in the economy in Ireland in the past ten years. More and more people are working in the media and media-related jobs.

The greatest expansion has probably been in public relations as Irish industry invests more in corporate communications.

The development of local radio has also contributed to expansion in jobs in the broadcasting side of the industry.

Legislative developments leading to a direct injection of funds to aid the independent television sector has meant that this is now a viable industry.

In direct response to this expansion, and to meet the popularity of the media as a career choice, there has been an explosion in the availability of journalism and media-related training courses.

JOBS

The National Union of Journalists represents over 3,000 people working in the media in Ireland, but the estimate of the number actually working in the industry is higher. If the independent television sector and all of public relations is taken into account, the number is probably nearer 5,000.

The NUJ's figures break down as follows:

- Newspapers   750
- Provincial Press   687
- Freelance   736
- Broadcasting   569
- PR/Information   336
- Magazines/Books   140

Of this 3,045, around 900 - nearly one third - are women.

The single biggest employers in the industry are the national daily papers and RTE.

But journalists are also to be found in local radio, the local press, magazines, trade magazines, public relations, both as consultants and in-house. They are to be found in government departments, voluntary groups, and working at home, as freelance writers, or producers.

The NUJ does not represent independent producers. SIPTU represents producers in RTE and some independents, but the independent sector operates largely in the self-employed category and is also difficult to measure, given its recent growth.

FREELANCING

A considerable number of the full-time journalists working in Ireland, whether in RTE, the national dailies and Sundays, as well as local radio and provincial press, began their careers as freelance journalists. And there are dozens of people working as full-time and part-time freelance writers, enjoying the freedom and independence of self-employment.

Doing a course does not guarantee a job and freelancing means building experience, making contacts and getting published - or broadcast - while waiting for a vacancy. But a recognised training course is invaluable in learning the basic skills from scratch.

Freelance journalists are to be found everywhere, but mostly in Dublin. It's the only part of the Republic where the industry is big enough to give a living to a large number of freelances.

Freelances are to be found in the newsrooms of RTE and the national dailies, evenings and Sundays, doing casual but probably regular shifts and filling the inevitable gaps caused by illness, holidays and natural wastage.

They are to be found writing the feature pages of the evening papers and the daily papers.

Their work fills the pages of all the Irish women's magazines.

They are to be found in the courts all over the city, filing copy to evening and daily papers, and as "stringers" for English and international papers.

Freelance journalists will find work writing for trade magazines, turning advertising material into readable copy.

And freelance journalists turn their hands to film, theatre and book reviews, colour, opinion columns and supplying foreign news outlets when an Irish story hits the world headlines.

Many of the photographers whose pictures liven up the front pages are freelancers, doing occasional or regular news shifts for the photo editor of a national daily or Sunday paper.

JOBS IN BROADCASTING

RTE RADIO AND TELEVISION

RTE is the biggest employer of broadcasting staff in Ireland, and there is a steady demand for staff there.

The RTE newsroom has advertised for journalists on several occasions over the past number of years, with an estimated 30 new journalists joining the newsroom in the past four years. This has been due to the expansion in news output, creating new jobs, and the high mobility rate among experienced newsroom journalists.

RTE has recruited directly from the Journalism schools, from local radio in increasing numbers, from the ranks of freelance journalists and from newspapers, particularly the *Irish* and *Evening Press*.

Other competitions in RTE have been for producers in Radio, and for producer-directors in Television. Many of these vacancies are filled in-house, and others come from the professions of teaching, the arts and independent film-making.

"For the job of journalist, we are not going to take someone directly from school or college," said Monica Clune, head of Appointments and Staff Development in RTE. "Some experience is necessary, and in general, a third level qualification. The ability to research, write and have news judgement is necessary for any of the journalistic jobs in RTE."

All RTE recruitment is advertised in the *RTE Guide*, on the Aertel service, and in the national newspapers, under the terms of the Broadcasting Acts, and staff contracts are only awarded from applications received through public competitions. RTE generally offers one-year contracts at first, followed by continuous employment after a number of years; since the mid-1980s, permanent staff appointments have not been made.

Vacancies are competitively sought. Over 1,500 applied for the position of trainee television Producer/Director in 1994, for a handful of places on a training course. More than 400 applied for a recent Journalists' panel for the newsroom.

RTE, with nearly 2,000 staff, fills vacancies for everything from administrative positions, to musicians for the orchestra, actors for radio drama and reporters for the newsroom.

As well as staff contracts, individual programmes and departments sometimes make temporary contracts available on a short-term basis to fill temporary staff shortages.

In Local Radio, journalists are recruited from journalism courses - when a short placement can often lead to a job - from the ranks of freelance journalists and from local contacts.

THE PRINT MEDIA

Newsrooms of daily and Sunday newspapers house a combination of staff journalists and freelance reporters.

Daily newspapers recruit from the existing pool of experienced freelance staff, tried and trusted from months and sometimes years of freelance news shifts and feature writing for the paper.

Newspapers also advertise for reporters from time to time. Staff are recruited from other national newspapers, from provincial papers and from the specialist press.

Many journalists now come from the two main training courses in the College of Commerce in Rathmines and in Dublin City University. Each year, about 20 are trained in each course, do a work experience placement and then work as freelances or get a full time job.

Many people become journalists through different routes; photographers and writers offer ideas and work to commissioning editors at features and news level; all news editors and features editors in newspapers and magazines are constantly trying out new people.

Many people leave one profession to become a journalist; former teachers are good examples; many come in either by doing a training course, or by building up a body of freelance work. Teachers often bring a specialist knowledge of finance, science, or the arts with them, which is invaluable in specialist journalism in particular.

SUPPORT STAFF

National newspapers in particular have a range of support staff bringing out the newspaper.

Printing Staff

in the printroom layout the pages from the maps provided by the subeditors; they run the printing presses, ensure all the elements are in place and ensure the paper is ready for distribution on time.

Graphic Artists

include cartoonists who provide the light relief and satirical comment in the newspaper, and those who design the graphics such as maps, and graphics, to illustrate a story. They generally work on a freelance basis.

Copytakers

are the typists who take in the telephoned copy from reporters in the field, freelance regional reporters and foreign writers. Their copy is sent directly to the onscreen layout, where it is subbed and placed.

Librarians

are the people who run the newsroom cuttings and reference libraries for journalists. Copies of their own newspapers are kept, as well as newspaper cuttings on related matters.

Columnists

can include non-journalist specialists who write opinion for the newspapers; generally they come from the professional world, although some are existing journalists within the newspaper.

JOB DESCRIPTIONS:

The Reporter

the main writer of the newspaper; gets the information and writes it up as a news story; follows up stories or angles on stories; conducts interviews; writes features.

The Sub Editor

takes the journalists' copy, checks for accuracy, makes it ready for layout; writes crossheads (the small headline down the column) and headlines.

The Photographer

provides the visual angle to a news story or feature. Often tells the whole story with a single photograph. Is an essential part of the newspaper.

The News Editor

is the linchpin of the newsroom and is probably the one person who knows where everyone is and what they are doing. Decides what stories will be covered that day. Assigns reporters to cover stories. Draws up daily "diary" list based on notifications sent by post and follow-ups to running stories.

The Editor

co-ordinates and oversees the running of the paper. Writes editorials as do senior staff such as correspondents. Decides editorial policy.

BROADCASTING

The Reporter

records the information on tape, and broadcasts the story on radio, or, if working on television, works with a camera crew and editor to devise a visual and aural story ready for broadcast.

RTE describes the job of its news journalist as "to gather news for broadcasting on both radio and television. He/she has also to prepare and present news bulletins, accurate and objective news reports from the facts gathered, as well as to interview on sound and/or vision persons who are in the news".

The News Editor

prepares the diary of the day, and assigns reporters and crews to chosen stories for the bulletins and main news programmes.

The Programme Editor

like a producer on radio or television programmes, co-ordinates the items for broadcast on the day in conjunction with the presenter and reporters. Decides what goes into the programme.

The Videotape Editor

a technical role, working with the reporter using technology to edit pictures with sound and "cut a package" ready for broadcast.

The Television Producer/Director

the "captain of the starship" in studio, co-ordinating all the sources of material, recorded and live, working a few minutes ahead while still keeping an eye on the live output. Nerves of steel required.

RTE describes this job as "the leader of the creative team involved in programme-making with primary responsibility for the formulation, production and direction of television programmes, and for the management of the technical and financial resources assigned to him/her".

The Floor Manager

literally, in charge of what moves on the studio floor. Connected by headset to the Director, he/she passes on directions and counts down live inserts. He/she is the presenter's umbilical cord, connecting him or her to the director/producer at the control desk, giving information on time and items.

The Presenter

the anchor or front person for television and radio programmes, and the central voice and image of the programme. Television programme presenters need to be calm, with a pleasant manner, an ability to be able to deal with broadcast technology, and a good grasp of current affairs.

The Researcher

initiates ideas, co-ordinates audiences where required, writes up briefing material on guests, items and books for the presenter. A valuable resource to any programme.

RTE describes the job as "involving the preparation of advance briefs for producers, contact with contributors, and assembly of documentary and audio/visual material for programme use".

The Radio Producer

is the team leader and creative person, who decides the overall content of a programme, leads a team of researchers and reporters, as well as overseeing the technical requirements of the programme. Has a research role also, and directs the programme from the control desk to the presenter.

Sound Operator

a job that is changing with new audio technology, the sound operator works from the control desk, ensuring sound quality, preparing tapes, putting on the commercial breaks, and ensuring the sound studio is prepared for the programme's transmission. Also works on outside broadcasts, and in recording of live music, as well as doing sound supervision on radio documentaries. Works closely with the programme's producer.

Broadcasting Assistant

the administrative backup for the programme team, in charge of logging music, taking calls from the public, and providing office and administrative services to the team.

PUBLIC RELATIONS

Jobs in the public relations industry can be roughly divided into two sectors: in house and consultancy.

"In house" is where a company develops its own internal Public Relations Unit. Depending on the size of the company this can include a Press and Public relations officer, who liaises with the media and develops a public relations strategy; an information officer who is responsible for publications and internal communications such as newsletters and assistants or deputies.

In Ireland the number of companies with significant information units is small, and many are in the semi-state sector. Some, but not many, Government departments run fully-staffed press and information offices, often run by full-time, redeployed civil servants.

But small companies, or voluntary groups, can often afford to employ only one person to do everything.

The other option is to hire in a public relations consultant.

Public relations consultancy is a growing part of the media industry. The number of companies employing more than ten people is very small. The vast majority are small, with two to five people working in the company. Like the rest of the media industry, it is concentrated in Dublin.

The Press Officer

liaises with the media, answers queries, supplies information, sets up press conferences, writes and distributes press releases, gives briefings, provides advice.

The Public Relations Consultant

sets up media "events" such as photocalls, press conferences, publicises events for clients, advises on publicity, and briefs journalists and programme makers on client's requirements.

PUBLISHING

There are over 140 publishing houses in Ireland, although most of them are small, with fewer than four people working there. Clé, the Irish Publishers Association, runs courses in publishing.

GETTING A JOB IN THE MEDIA

What Makes a Good Journalist?

There is no one quality which on its own, guarantees success as a journalist.

Intelligence and the ability to write clearly and concisely is important.

Interest in news and current affairs, as well as an enquiring mind and a basic curiosity about how things work and why is also the hallmark of a good journalist.

Dedication is essential. Being interested in people and the stories they have to tell makes for a good reporter.

A good broadcaster is born, not made, in that voice quality is essential.

Being organised and disciplined is necessary for success as a public relations consultant.

Intelligence and creativity, a mind brimming with ideas, is essential to the making of a producer.

We asked a selection of journalists what they thought were the essential qualities needed to be a good reporter:

Martin Breheny – G.A.A. Correspondent for the Sunday Press

"A nose for a story, and concentration, that's what makes a good reporter. Sometimes it is very difficult to watch a match closely with everything going on around you. You need to have the attention to detail, and be able to form your own opinion to be a good sports journalist."

Veronica Guerin – Investigative Journalist

"I think tenacity, and the ability to listen, are the two essential qualities of a good journalist. You have got to be prepared to work long hours, to keep making phone calls to get your story. And you have to genuinely like people, all the time you are dealing with them in this job - you have got to be able to break the ice with them."

Don Buckley – Assistant Editor in the Irish Times

"Energy and enthusiasm - those are the qualities I look for in a reporter. And persistence - not giving up, and getting around the obstacles of a story."

Mary Raftery – Current Affairs Television Producer in RTE

"An enquiring mind and a creative mind is what marks a good journalist in my opinion. In the job I'm in it also requires a good visual sense - being able to see how a story which is facts based can be turned into an item for viewers, not readers. But in the first instance it's the asking "why" which is most important in the making of a good reporter."

Eamonn Farrell – Photographer

"A thick neck is an essential requirement to be a press photographer. And you need to be committed; if you really want to do the job properly, you have to sacrifice a lot of time and other interests. And you need to have an understanding partner. There are easier ways of making a living, but there is a great buzz out of it when it goes well."

GETTING THE JOB - WHAT THE EMPLOYERS SAY

The RTE Newsroom

Joe Mulholland is Director of News, RTE, and has interviewed most of the 30 successful applicants for jobs in the newsroom over the last few years. This is what he has to say about what he's looking for in an applicant:

"Firstly we look for a high level of intelligence, the ability to grasp any subject matter, because they will be working as general reporters for quite a while. Broadcasting ability, a good voice, and good appearance are important because newsroom journalists work in both media. However, we do place ability, intelligence and to some extent educational experience high on the agenda too. To have credibility and authority on air is important. But we have not allowed youth to stand in the way of recruitment. We are willing to invest time and training in someone if we feel they have the potential to develop."

The Provincial Newspaper

Vicki Weller is Editor of the *Leinster Leader.*

"We don't recruit from any one single source. We have had placements from the journalism colleges, and we have also advertised for journalists from time to time. The people we have had working for us have come from various backgrounds – University, Rathmines, DCU.

There is also a certain amount of the "local connection" involved. All but two of the nine reporters involved in the paper at the moment are from the area or have connections with the area. That's inevitable. Of course all have their qualifications and had experience before they came here. In an interview situation, local connections help. Nowadays the demands of the job are such that someone who doesn't have the ability to get out there and do that job won't make it, no matter what their qualifications are."

The Freelance Writer

Maura O'Kiely is Editor of *U* magazine and depends for her copy on freelance journalists.

"The freelance journalist who approaches me must have good ideas - and lots of them. They must be able to sell me that idea, but what's more important is that they deliver on what they promise. So many don't. I get copy which is badly researched, badly written, slapdash, and late. I spend most of my time doing surgery on copy which comes into me. Getting basic facts right, such as how someone spells their name, is essential, but it's amazing how many basic errors I see. I like someone to be persistent - and if they are having problems with a piece, I like them to ring and discuss it with me. Then I know where I stand. And getting copy on disk is just magic!"

The Reporter

Peter Murtagh is Editor of the *Sunday Tribune.*

"There are always jobs for good reporters, especially young ones with energy and ideas. The ones who have the talent will always make it, even though it is difficult to get a job in journalism these days. I'm always looking out for new talent."

The Personnel Officer

Monica Clune is head of Appointments and Staff Development in RTE.

"When we get applications for jobs in RTE programmes, we look for evidence of motivation and commitment to journalism. People have be to capable of hard work, the ability to get on with people, and leadership qualities, as well as a good basic education, and a good ability to write and speak English."

RTE'S ENTRY REQUIREMENTS

As the largest employer of journalists and broadcasters in the country, public competitions for jobs attract thousands of applicants. RTE has a number of general entry requirements for programme-making jobs.

They expect a multitude of skills and talents, in concert with the ability to work with and use sophisticated technology.

In general, a third level qualification is needed, usually to a high standard.

Although RTE does run some in-house training courses, it expects applicants to have the basic skills already acquired, as well as relevant experience.

Candidates should be able to work in Irish, and a knowledge of European language is an advantage.

Specialised knowledge in subjects that broadcasting covers is important, e.g. current affairs, light entertainment, education, young people, the arts, and religion, as well as a familiarity with contemporary Ireland.

Personal initiative and judgement are required in programme makers, as well as a creative ability to turn ideas into successful programmes.

GETTING INTO THE MEDIA: DOING A COURSE

Increasingly, young aspiring journalists are doing specialised training courses to get into the media.

There are now as many courses as there are people to set them up; evening courses and private colleges are increasingly offering media studies, broadcast journalism and training courses.

In this section, we list the main journalism courses available at post-Leaving Certificate, and post-graduate level.

A proven interest in the media is a huge advantage in applying for places on these courses.

Dublin Institute of Technology (DIT), Aungier Street. (Formerly College of Commerce, Rathmines)

■ *Certificate in Journalism*:

Fifteen years ago, this was the only journalism course available at third level. It's a two-year certificate course; very competitive entry requirements. Portfolio needed. Most students go on to be full time journalists.

Minimum entry requirements include two Honours subjects at Leaving Certificate, grade HC3 or higher, and selection is based on points. It is a two-year course, and application is made through the CAO system.

■ *Communications Degree:*

This degree level course requires at least two Honours at Leaving Certificate, and is four years' duration.

Senior College, Ballyfermot, Dublin, – Post Leaving Certificate Course in Media related subjects:

(Mature students who may not have the entry requirements are welcome to apply; relevant experience will be taken into consideration. Applicants for courses in media and broadcasting are interviewed in May. Summer school courses in radio and television are held between June and August.)

■ *National Diploma in Broadcasting and Journalism:*

This UK recognised course is a two-year full-time course aimed at giving students an understanding of media techniques and production skills in Radio, Television/Video and Print Journalism. Course content includes print editing, production, radio tape recording, print origination and sound industries.

Entry requirements include a proven interest in the media, a Leaving Certificate with passes in five subjects including English.

■ *Higher Diploma in Radio Production and Journalism:*

A new full-time two-year programme covering all aspects of radio production, including work experience in SCB FM, the senior college's own radio station.

Entry requirements include a proven interest in radio, two HC2s at Higher Level preferably including English, plus four other passes at Leaving Certificate level. Applicants are also required to submit a practical example of their journalistic work.

■ *Certificate in Print Media and Journalism:*

This one-year course aims to provide a foundation in the skills needed for further study in print journalism and the media.

Entry requirements include five passes in the Leaving Certificate, including English, and a proven interest in the media.

■ *Higher National Diploma in Print Journalism and Media Management:*

This two-year full-time course specialises in the practical skills of print journalism, including writing, subbing, production, press photography and desktop publishing.

Entry requirements include two HC2s which must include English, plus four other passes at Leaving Certificate or equivalent.

■ *Diploma in Television Operations and Production:*

This two-year course provides a general knowledge of, and training in, the various operations of television production, with extensive practical experience, including working in a television studio and post production facilities equipped to broadcast standards.

Entry requirements include a Leaving Certificate with passes in five subjects. Applicants should submit a portfolio at interview stage demonstrating good camera technique.

Dublin City University, Glasnevin, Dublin

■ *B.A. in Journalism*

This four-year degree is designed to provide a broad general education along with a number of specific subjects and key professional skills appropriate to graduates who choose journalism as a career. The course covers the French and German languages, practical journalism skills, media analysis, as well as one term in a French or German speaking country gaining practical educational and media experience.

Minimum entry requirements include Leaving Certificate with grade C3 in two Higher or Common Level subjects and grade D3 in four Ordinary, Common or Higher Level subjects. Applicants must also have at least a grade C3 in Higher Level French or German together with at least a grade C3 in Higher Level English.

■ *B.A. in Communication Studies*

This three-year course combines the theoretical and the practical, covering communications and psychology, as well as video production, radio production and photography and print. Keyboard

skills are taught, and a final year research project constitutes one-third of the total marks for the award of the degree.

Minimum entry requirements include Leaving Certificate with grade C3 in two Higher or Common Level subjects, and grade D3 in four Ordinary, Common or Higher level subjects. A grade C3 in Higher Level English is also required.

■ *M.A. in Journalism.*

This one-year course aims to ensure the rapid development of a range of professional journalistic skills, as well as equipping students with a detailed knowledge of the structure and function of the media industry. Subjects covered include news reporting, feature writing, broadcast journalism, media law, and media history and structure, as well as workshops in radio skills, television skills and photography. As well as doing a major project, students also take part in a summer placement in a media workplace.

Applicants should have a good Honours degree (2.2 or better), and there are some places available for older students with relevant experience. Applicants must have a minimum of 40 words per minute typing speed, and a short list of applicants is interviewed.

University College Galway

■ *Post-Graduate Higher Diploma in Applied Communications*:

This one-year full time course covers print journalism, radio journalism and public relations.

Graduates of UCG and other colleges are eligible; a general degree is eligible, plus good portfolios of journalistic work. Most graduates go onto local radio and provincial press jobs, or freelance at national level.

Applicants are assessed on the basis of their degree in conjunction with their portfolio, or other evidence of interest in, and suitability to, a career in communications, as well as an interview.

Dun Laoghaire College of Art and Design

■ *National Certificate in Radio Broadcasting:*

This new qualification is a two-year full-time course, with places for 20 to 25 students. Recognised by the NCEA, applicants need a minimum grade D in five subjects in the Leaving Certificate, including English; they must present a portfolio of relevant written or audio work, and must do an interview after initial portfolio screening.

Students will get a solid foundation in the principles and techniques of radio broadcasting to the level of producer, and complete a portfolio of printed materials and completed programmes demonstrating a wide range of broadcasting skills.

DIT Aungier Street (Former College of Commerce) Dublin. Tel. 01 478 5252

■ *Diploma in Public Relations*

Recognised by the Public Relations Institute of Ireland and the Institute of Public Relations (UK), as the educational standard required for full membership of each institute, combined with relevant professional experience, this is one of the main courses of its kind for working in PR in Ireland.

Entry requirements include a third level qualification, equal to or higher than a two-year full-time certificate with credit or distinction. Applications are not accepted from school leavers.

Also there are a number of evening and private college courses in Public Relations. Before applying, contact the Public Relations Institute of Ireland to see if the course is recognised. Tel. 01 661 8004.

ANNE MARIE SMYTH, NEWS REPORTER

The Power of Words

Belfast-born Anne Marie Smyth always wanted to be a journalist. She just never envisaged she'd be working either in Dublin or in broadcasting.

Still in her first year in RTE, she was recruited as a newsroom reporter from the *Evening Press*, just a few years out of the Dublin City University's post-graduate Journalism course.

After a year studying Architecture in Queen's University Belfast, she switched to History and Politics - a natural road into journalism.

She became the editor of the student newspaper, *Press Release,* the highlight of which was interviewing film makers Alan Parker and David Puttnam.

Having failed to get on the Thomson Group's Trainee Journalist course through the *Belfast Telegraph*, she was offered a place on the DCU course, due to a good portfolio of student work. "This previous experience was vital, because it showed that I was seriously interested in journalism. Over 1,000 applied for the 20 places on the course that year."

A work experience placement in *The Sunday Tribune* was invaluable for experience and published material, and she remained on a freelance contract with the paper for a further year and a half; during that time she covered the release of the Guildford Four, and got

the first interview with Paul Hill, wrote features and profiles, the TV column, and news stories on the juvenile justice issue.

During a freelance period after leaving the *Tribune*, she reported on her visit to a Romanian orphanage for the *Irish Times*, and began writing for the *Sunday* and *Evening Press*. She was recruited as a news reporter with the *Evening Press*, her first staff job.

She remained there for two years before moving to the RTE newsroom in 1994, a year after getting on a reporters' panel following a successful interview and screen test.

"I'd always been interested in broadcasting, and now I am working in the TV and radio newsroom. I've worked on the News at One, on Morning Ireland, and on the Radio subs desk, where I've written the bulletins. I'm currently on the TV subs desk, doing TV production and bulletins; cutting pictures to go with the stories that the newsreader reads, and putting news packages together when the reporter is out on a story."

She's also done a stint in the Oireachtas unit, covering the proceedings into the committee investigating the break-up of the Fianna Fail-Labour government.

Her advice to aspiring journalists? "Get experience,

and if in college, do student journalism. Get your writing published."

Is the reality of journalism what she had expected?

"I cannot imagine doing anything else. Every day is different to the previous one. In the *Evening Press*, I have interviewed everyone from drug pushers, to people who have just lost a son or daughter. People can be surprisingly helpful in those situations. Journalism gives you a very different perspective on life. One day it's Linford Christie you're talking to, the next day it's someone who's had an organ transplant."

And what kind of people are best suited to journalism?

"There is a perception that a brass neck is needed, but that's not necessary. Your neck can get harder as a result, but a degree of sensitivity makes you a better listener. You need to have an appreciation of words and the power of words that can be put simply but with a powerful message."

"There is a certain element of luck in getting the story. You cannot bargain for that, but you need to know when you are being lucky so that you can actually capitalise on it."

MARY MULVIHILL, FREELANCE JOURNALIST

The Self-Employed Science Writer

There are not many fully qualified geneticists working as freelance journalists in Ireland, but Mary Mulvihill has found a niche for one.

Specialising in Genetics, with a degree in Biology led Mary to become a research scientist for Teagasc. There, from time to time, she wrote articles for the farming press on the research there.

A natural communicator with an ability to explain science to the non-scientist, she realised research was not for her, but still loved science.

When redundancies were being offered, someone suggested the DCU course in Journalism, and she jumped at the idea.

"It was a bit of a risk, but I decided to try it. It was intensive, but I found it invaluable in teaching me the basic skills of journalism."

She planned to be a freelance from the start. "Being realistic I knew there wasn't a full time job in it - no Irish paper has a full-time specialist in that area - the level of science coverage is too low."

Over six years on, she now has a number of regular outlets and new opportunities are coming up. She is joint editor of *Technology Ireland* magazine, writes for *The Irish Times*, and does science slots for Radio One's Pat Kenny Show. She's also working on a 15-minute science programme for RTE Radio One. She covers Irish scientific developments for the "New Scientist" and "Nature" magazines.

"The *Technology Ireland* work is the safety net for me," she said. "It takes up half my time for 10 months of the year and is a regular source of income. Freelancing is a very insecure existence. A regular slot somewhere is vital."

Freelancing never gets easy, she believes. There is the constant pressure to earn, to come up with ideas, to find new markets.

"You are only as good as your last piece," she said. "You are always trying to do something new, and keep your name up front."

She works from her home near Dublin's city centre, with a personal computer and a telephone. She's also got an invaluable answering machine, and has a fax and modem installed into her computer. She needs to be accessible all the time.

She spends at least one day a week keeping up to date with the latest developments, reading international papers, science magazines she has subscribed to.

And she spends a lot of time on the telephone. "In terms of developing a speciality, you need to keep up to date with your contacts."

Freelance Journalist, Mary Mulvihill works from home.   *Photograph: Kate Horgan.*

"You need to manage your time very well, that's something I have learned over the years," she said. "You need to be disciplined, to schedule your work. There are lots of distractions working from home. "

"Isolation is a disadvantage of the freelance life," she said. "Sometimes the office structure can be important to break that isolation. That's where *Technology Ireland* is important, because it gives me an office structure for some time every month."

The other main disadvantage is earning potential.

"For the hours and work I do, I should be getting a much higher income. I am not earning anything like what I would be earning in a full time job."

But there is great scope to her speciality. She's thinking towards a TV series, has an idea for a book, and is researching an idea for a science exhibition.

While discipline and good time management are vital, she also believes being creative in finding new markets is also central. "I always have more ideas than I can hope to place."

BRIAN DOWLING, THE POLITICAL REPORTER

Sitting on the Sidelines of History

"It's the sense of being on the margins of history, of being there when history is made"

This is the source of the fascination of being a political writer, of being on duty all the time, of working nights and Sundays as a matter of course, and of spending one's working life in the hothouse atmosphere of Leinster House.

After 15 years as a journalist, Brian Dowling has reached what many would consider to be the pinnacle of any journalist's ambition - the Pol Corrs (political correspondents) Room on the second floor of Leinster House.

Here a select group which reports and comments on the comings and goings of the Government and opposition, works out of two rooms and one studio (for RTE), wanders the corridors, the bar and the canteen, talking to politicians, gauging opinion and gathering stories - often leaked stories - for their readers.

"Essentially what the political staff do is write political stories, follow the trends, the machinations of government ministers and departments, follow the internal politics of parties, between parties and between the parties in the coalition, and comment on the broader economic, legal and constitutional issues as they arise".

Having graduated from Trinity College, Dubliner Dowling worked as a freelance journalist for a number of years.

"I started on the Dublin local papers and the freesheets and I gradually worked my way on to the *Irish Press.* Eventually I got a contract."

After six years with the *Irish Press* he joined the *Irish Independent* in 1989 as a general reporter. He had a short stint as Deputy Editor of the *Evening Herald* and was also Legal Affairs Correspondent before joining colleagues Gene McKenna and Chris Glennon on the political staff, based in Leinster House.

"I love it," he says.

Why?

"It's the sense of unpredictability. You just never know what's around the next corner. Politics has a buzz, an incredible sense of excitement about it. Even for those in the midst of the worst political nightmares, there is still that sense of excitement, that inexplicable attraction and exhilaration of the highs of remarkable achievements of politicians, such as the ceasefire. Then on the other hand you get to see, often close up, the same people self-destruct. It's just extraordinary."

PAT MONTAGUE, THE PUBLIC RELATIONS CONSULTANT

Not Just About Taking Journalists to Lunch

Pat Montague runs his own PR consultancy, Montague Communications. He is one of a large number of small operators in the PR consultancy business, having come to self-employment after a short stint in a Dublin-based PR consultancy company which had "head-hunted" him from his previous job as Youth Officer with the Labour Party.

Setting up on your own is very common in the PR business. Like other professions, relationships built up with clients forms the core of the business and many consultants will set up on their own once they have established a good client base.

Like many sole traders, Pat is able to keep his overheads down by running the business from home, in his case with the help of one assistant. His client base ranges from professional groups and organisations such as the Institute of Architects to agencies such as the Independent Radio and Television Commission to book publishers.

"It's not a job for the shy retiring type," says Pat. "You have to be able to get on the phone to a complete stranger, whether a client or a journalist and sell yourself and your ideas," he says.

And what does the job of the PR person involve?

"Despite what many people think, it's not about taking journalists to lunch!" Pat says he has only taken journalists to lunch, on behalf of clients, on two occasions, and on neither occasion did it result in coverage, good or bad.

"It makes an assumption about journalists which they are uncomfortable about - and that is, that somehow they can be bought."

So what does it take to be a successful PR consultant? Pat identifies the following: good writing and communications skills; creativity; organisational skills; a good manager of time; determination; and if you are a sole trader - a Business Plan.

Public Relations in fact involves a wide range of functions and skills, including the following: marketing a product; developing a profile for a company or organisation; event management; internal communications such as newsletters; communications training; public affairs - otherwise known as lobbying, – or ensuring that your clients views are heard when decisions are made.

PR Consultant, Pat Montague.

PROFILE

STEPHEN O'BYRNES, PRESS OFFICER

The Political Handler

When Stephen O'Byrnes got "the political call", as he calls it himself, from the newly formed Progressive Democrats in 1986, he felt he really had no choice but to take it.

At the time he was writing columns of political analysis for the *Irish Independent*, and the call was like a challenge. "Having doled out the medicine, it was a bit like: physician, heal thyself," as he puts it.

At that time, he had been a journalist for some 15 years. He entered journalism, like many others, by accident. A "passionate" interest in current affairs led directly to a degree in Modern Irish History in UCD and he started work in the *Irish Press* in 1970 "to keep me going while I was doing an MA". The MA never got finished, but the career in journalism certainly took off.

Twelve of those fifteen years were spent in the *Irish Press* - as subeditor, general reporter, feature writer, agricultural correspondent, consumer affairs correspondent and political writer.

Then he moved to Independent House as political columnist and News Analysis editor.

Stephen joined as Press Officer and Policy Director, but working for a small party "with very limited resources" means that he does just about everything - writing scripts, researching, initiating policy ideas, liaising with the media on a daily basis acting as advisor to the party leader on a range of things.

And taking phone calls at home at all hours of the day and night.

"I was and suppose I am a handler - although I think the title has developed a pejorative ring in recent times. Politicians whether they like it or not, must recognise that nowadays the medium is the message - and the most important media in terms of how people judge and form their perceptions, are radio and television. I see my role as ensuring that the people I work with cope with that. That often means developing the soundbite, the message in a format that suits radio and television. Increasingly the papers are led by radio and television anyway. The days of the five page script are gone. The soundbite is the thing," he says.

And yes, it helps to be committed to the party.

"Although I feel that the vast bulk of the work I do, as a professional, could be done for another party, I couldn't put in the hours I do if I wasn't committed. And it certainly is important to have a sympathy for the person or the party you are working for."

KATE HORGAN, FREELANCE PHOTOGRAPHER

Just One of the Boys

Kate Horgan is a freelance photographer, with five years experience. When I spoke to her, she'd just lost a regular three days work with a Sunday newspaper, due to budget cutbacks. She shrugged.

"I'd turned down other work to do this, I wasn't expecting it."

Kate knows that as a freelance in a small Dublin-based market, she can't be choosey. "I'd prefer to be doing news all the time, but I also do product launches for public relations companies, and things like that."

Her distinctive photographs of business events, like AGMs, or business launches for the *Sunday Business Post* has made her name. "The paper wanted something different anyway, and I am able to interpret a bit, which I like doing."

She has a lot of formal education with a B.A. in Communications from D.C.U. plus a Masters in Photography from the University of Minnesota in the U.S.

After a few years in the competitive environment of Seattle, she came home to try work here.

She taught photography, and built up a portfolio as a news photographer. During that time, she did a series of documentary photographs of the Bosnian community in Ireland for the *Sunday Tribune*, something she would like to do more of. "Features and news, that's the area I want to be in – preferably full time in a daily newspaper!

"You don't need a formal education to be a photographer. You can do it without thinking, but I like to think that photographs can educate people as much as words can."

Getting a regular shift in a newspaper is difficult in the beginning; most freelances build up a varied portfolio. A big help for her was getting shots of David Bowie at an unscheduled gig in the Baggot Inn in Dublin.

Although no photographers were allowed in, she got by with her camera in her bag, and took two rolls of film before the bouncers could get to her. "I sold them to the *Sunday World* and to *Hot Press*. It was a good example of having your camera with you when the opportunity arose. But now I don't bring my camera with me everywhere. You have to leave it at home sometimes, like when you're meeting your friends in a pub."

She works from home, with an answering machine and a bleep to back up her Nikon camera. "You need

Freelance Photographer, Kate Horgan.   Photograph: Conor Horgan.

to be a self-starter, and it takes time to get established. Build up a varied portfolio, with everything from a portrait of Christy Moore in his dressing-room before the gig to a hockey match," she advises.

She's a rarity, being a woman news photographer in a man's world.

"There's only one female staff news photographer at the moment." she said. 'There are plenty of women freelance reporters now, and I think it's only a matter of time before you see more women photographers, because at student level, it's about 50-50."

In the beginning, at big news "scrums" where photographers pushed and shoved for the best angle. Kate found the lads behaved like gentlemen. "They were a bit paternal, giving me rolls of film and that. But then they got used to me, and now I'm the same as the rest of them."

11 SUPERHIGHWAYS & SATELLITES

The Future and the Media

"The world isn't run by weapons anymore, or energy or money. It's run by little ones and zeroes. Little bits of data. It's all just electrons."

Cosmo, in the film *Sneakers*.

Technology has brought change so fast in the past few years, that nobody can keep up with the latest developments. The potential is vast as the three technologies of telephone, television and computer come together in a new information age.

Suffice it to say that while the notebook and the telephone remain the mainstay of the ordinary journalist, the technology available to get the news across has reached an unprecedented level of transition. The notebook could soon be an electronic one; the telephone may have a picture attached by the beginning of the next century. And work practices are likely to change dramatically.

Print and broadcasting journalists alike are set to gain from the introduction in the next few years of satellite technology, as fibre-optic cables and digital sound allow the transmission and retrieval of information in many forms. Satellites will be the most important medium of transmission of pictures and sound around the world, aided by digitalised information on fibre-optic cables linking the journalist at the South Pole to her office in south county Dublin.

The world will be linked by an information network of cables encircling the globe.

CHANGE ONE: THE PRINTING PRESS

In the mid-80s, there was a technological revolution in the print industry. Most newspapers at national and local level have now introduced what's known as "new technology" into their newsrooms. Since the 80s, noisy typewriters have been replaced by computer screens and laptops, and increasingly, journalists outside the office are filing copy down telephone lines from their portable computers, instead of reading them over the line to a copytaker.

Journalists at their desks now input their stories directly to the central computer typesetter, and many printers' jobs have been eliminated. By the end of the century, it is likely that most newspapers will have moved to the full-page, on-screen make up system, virtually eliminating the role of printers who paste down strips of bromide copy from the photosetter onto a page for printing.

Journalists' personal computers have also become their databases, accessible as online search systems for library information, and storage for their contacts.

CHANGE TWO: THE TELEPHONE

The Telephone and the Fibre-Optic Cable

It used to be the instrument for talking to someone; now it's a line to unlimited information.

A telephone line, on a fibre-optic cable, can send a

huge variety of video and audio information to the user. This fibre-optic cable can bring untold amounts of information - the voice, computer information and video information - down the line into your computer, or your television. The fibre in the cable is just the width of human hair and is made of glass, and it's under the street outside your house; experts say that a typical fibre-optic cable will contain 96 fibres; each pair of fibres is capable of transmitting 93,000 phone calls, or up to 20 channels of information simultaneously.

Then there's ISDN - short for Integrated Services Digital Network. Simply, this is a more sophisticated digitalised telephone line, on which fax, telex and voice can be sent more quickly, and with greater quality than before. The main benefits are speed: because of the purity of the digital lines, faxes are clearer and faster. And electronic transfer of files of data, voice, text and images will be faster and more secure.

The Mobile Phone

Once the preserve of London yuppies in wine bars, the mobile phone is now an essential tool of journalists. Much more adaptable with the use of satellite technology, the mobile can be used to reach people on the other side of the world, or in the local pub, and brings the journalist's latest news straight to the news editor's desk, or onto the radio.

CHANGE THREE: THE INTERNET AND THE INFORMATION SUPERHIGHWAY

This is a worldwide network of computers that share, store and pass on information. Everything from university libraries, and academic journals to the latest business information can be downloaded onto a personal computer, through a telephone line.

On the Internet, the user can send electronic mail, download information on a huge range of topics, and get software, not to mention "chatting" to people anywhere.

Although still much smaller at European level than in America, the Internet is becoming a valuable source of information on an unthinkable range of topics.

CHANGE FOUR: RADIO AND NEW TECHNOLOGY

With the new wave of digital computers comes digital sound. New technologies for recording and storing music and sound are being introduced in the 90s; a mini-disk, which can store dozens of songs, in a digital fashion, and the CD-rom, on which huge amounts of music can be kept, are changing audio technology.

The current system of recording and editing sound on tape will soon end; digital recording and editing, where sound is stored on hard disk in a computer is the method of the future. Already parts of the RTE

Radio service are using digital editing and recording.

And the system of transmission is also due to change. Currently, radio signals are broadcast by and large by transmitters sited at suitable locations around the country; this system will soon be replaced by the transmission of audio signals by satellite dish. Already, RTE is using the Astra satellite to beam its radio signal throughout western Europe.

It's also possible to get digital radio by TV cable. Since 1994, a company in Cavan has been providing a digital cable radio service; Cablelink in Dublin is looking at the possibilities of offering this different kind of radio: the subscriber decides what he or she wants to listen to, whether it's jazz, pop or classical. Already 30 channels are available, and the choice is likely to grow. The pre-recorded channels are transmitted by satellite from Atlanta, in the USA, to a London-based company, who send it further by satellite to the cable companies who then put it down the cable.

CHANGE FIVE: THE SATELLITE AND SATELLITE TELEVISION

What is a communications satellite? It's a station, that looks a bit like a dish, placed in orbit around the Earth to provide transmission channels for traffic to be transmitted over great distances. The satellite station's antennae can receive radio beams from an earth station transmitter, and retransmit the signals to another earth station - such as the dish in your back garden.

A worldwide system of satellites is now in place, and it's possible to transmit signals around the globe by bouncing them from one satellite to an earth station, and thence to another satellite. Mostly, they're used for television, voice, fax, and data transmission.

For reporters and programme makers, the use of a small van with a dish on top is enough to bring live television pictures onto domestic televisions from anywhere. For radio, it removes the limitations of mountains, and geographical obstacles to transmission of radio signals. It is making news instantaneous.

In Somalia, famine coverage was provided by some TV companies using portable satellite dishes, and aid workers kept in touch with home using portable satellite phones, attached to battery packs.

INTERACTIVE MULTI-MEDIA TV

Television as you've never seen it before will soon be in your sitting room, if the engineers have their way. It will look and sound different, and it will be able to provide a lot more services.

High Definition TV will be a flat screen, like a wall painting; it will give you details of your diary for that day, for example. You can download information onto it, like a computer. You can call up your video library and order a video, which will appear on the screen.

You can do your shopping on it; have a video conference with your office, and read your electronic mail.

And the television will be interactive - you'll be able to choose the camera angles on a GAA game, for example, call up statistics, have a live replay.

CHANGE SIX: PHOTOGRAPHY

Already, computerised newsrooms are transferring their whole photographic services to digital computer. Soon darkroom technicians could be a thing of the past, as computer scanning takes over the processing and printing of photographs. Newsrooms around the world can now receive photographs by digital computer from anywhere in the world, and put them straight onto the page; newspaper libraries and archives will be easily accessed from CD storage, and eventually, computerised cameras will take photographs, which can be instantly plugged into the computer and sent directly to the page make-up system.

CHANGING ALL THE TIME

Even as this chapter is being written, new technological developments are on the way. The storage and transfer of information is at the centre of the new technology. For journalists and all working in the communications industry, the next decade could be one of the most transitional since the telephone was invented.

PROFILE

LORNA SIGGINS

Satellite Technology in Action

How do you get your story to your Dublin newsroom when you're sitting in the middle of an African refugee camp, or on a remote Himalayan mountainside, miles from anything that remotely resembles civilisation?

In the past, journalists sent copy back through Army networks when they covered wars, or posted reports back, or, occasionally, used camels.

Nowadays, it's the sky and the technology up in space that comes to their rescue, i.e. satellites.

In 1993 *Irish Times* reporter Lorna Siggins climbed to Everest with the Irish Everest Expedition to send back regular reports to D'Olier Street. In the group was a portable satellite phone, which Lorna used via the Inmarsat satellite over the Indian Ocean to send her regular reports. So good was the technology that she was able to type her copy directly into a small portable laptop computer, link it to the satellite phone, press a button and the copy arrived a few seconds later in the *Irish Times* news computer.

"The laptop was programmed to communicate with the Inmarsat satellite, and transmit the text directly to the *Irish Times* computer in Dublin. So within seconds of dialling the number on the laptop, several hundred words of text was sent directly into the system in the office. It all worked a dream."

Most of the time, that is. Late into the climb, the generator that powered the satellite phone began to develop an altitude sickness.

"The generator also used the phone to broadcast onto the Pat Kenny radio show on RTE every week as well, and it was terrific. But the generator didn't like the high altitudes as we got nearer the top. But most of the time it worked."

Using satellites, the satellite phones though, is fairly rare for Irish journalists abroad, because of the expense. A small portable satellite telephone the size of a large suitcase, can cost several thousand pounds, and then there's the cost of using the satellite itself.

But international news companies like CNN and BBC now equip their foreign crews and reporters with satellite dishes as a norm. Crews carry the satellites that can beam their pictures around the world instantly. It makes the world a much smaller place.

Lorna Siggins of The Irish Times sends copy from Everest by Laptop and satellite phone.
Photograph: Courtesy of The Irish Himalayan Expedition.

EAMONN FARRELL, PHOTOGRAPHER

Putting Faces on the News

Dublin photographer Eamonn Farrell is one of the founders of Photocall, a news and features photo agency, one of just four established agencies in Dublin. He takes photographs for everyone from the *New York Times* to the daily Irish newspapers, to the *Garda Review*, and you'll see him, or one of his two agency colleagues, at most of the major news events around the city.

"We go to everything. Even if we are not commissioned, we have to have the shots for our clients. You can't just say you don't have a photograph of the riots in Lansdowne Road. They expect you to have one."

With a big archive of older material, plus current events and availability to cover stories, the Photocall agency is available around the clock.

Eamonn set up the agency in the Seventies with his brother Brian, also a press photographer. In the beginning, they knew nothing about getting photos of politicians.

"I remember ringing up a political party and saying we wanted stock shots of their TDs for our files. We came to Leinster House the following day, and they were all lined up waiting to be photographed. We couldn't believe it."

That has changed now - but as well, the technology has changed radically.

Now Eamonn is more likely to put his photographs on hard disk for a computer rather than printing them and sending the hard copy.

With the latest in communication technology in his city centre office, on a humming computer in touch with newsdesks around the world, his staff can send a photograph down the telephone line at the touch of a button.

"We can take pictures, transfer them to hard disk, and send them by modem, floppy disk or syquest in a matter of minutes," he says. Already one of his bigger clients is getting his regular black and white news photographs on a floppy disk.

"Cameras are becoming computers. We'll be able to plug them directly into a computer and press a button, with no printing or anything. It's all changing so fast it's unbelievable."

But the job of taking the photograph never changes.

He agrees that photographers sometimes have a more difficult job in sensitive times, because they are more visible than reporters.

"Yes, you can't just put the camera away. Certainly

Photographer Eamonn Farrell in the Photocall office.   Photograph: Leon Farrell.

events like private funerals can be difficult, but news editors put the photographers under huge pressure to get as close as possible. I think that if there's huge public interest in a story, then the photographers are there on their behalf."

Being a self-employed photographer in the small Dublin market is very competitive.

"It's a hard grind. You work very hard to make a living, and there has to be a huge investment in new technology if you want to serve the international market. The pressure is immense, they want everything so fast, immediately you've taken the shot. There's no time for reflection."

In the beginning, Eamonn was drawn to be a photographer by the example of Vietnam War photographer Don McCullin. "Those photographs were such powerful images. I wanted to be able to do that."

But a freelance existence rarely means time for reflection. Breaks have to be planned well in advance, and there's always the danger of missing something. "I want to go away a few times a year, to take photographs without a deadline, with time to think, and to capture that powerful image."

JOHN STERNE, ELECTRONIC JOURNALIST

Is this the Journalism of the Future?

Every Monday morning, hundreds of business people use their computers to get their latest news. Instead of buying a weekly magazine, these readers get their latest computing news from their computer - by e-mail, or electronic mail.

This could be the form of newspapers for the future - written directly onto a computer screen, and transmitted electronically onto the subscriber's computer screen. No paper, no ink.

Journalist John Sterne is the editor of "It's Monday." He works from the front room of his house in Dublin's south inner city. From there, he has a computer - an Apple Power Macintosh, along with a fax modem, two telephones, an answering machine, a second PC, and a portable laptop computer.

Three years old, Sterne founded the electronic magazine to fill a gap: there was nobody doing news on computer and telecommunications developments in the Irish media, despite the demand. He knew this audience could be reached by e-mail.

Every Sunday, the pages of news, about 6,000 words in all, are sent to his subscribers. "It takes about 70 minutes to get it through the service provider to all the addresses."

Sterne has been a freelance journalist for 14 years, starting as a travel writer before discovering computing and new technology. He wrote for *Business and Finance*, and *Irish Computer Magazine,* the *Sunday Tribune* and international outlets.

"Typically, I write a string of stories - the latest computer software from Microsoft, for example, courses on Information Technology for students, a diary of events in the business. It's an electronic news service."

Most of his subscribers are in software companies, or related industries, as well as semi-state industries, computer manufacturers and large organisations. Over 200 organisations are licenced to receive "It's Monday" each week.

"Most organisations have e-mail, with an external gateway," he says. "But anyone with a personal computer and a modem can use it."

Is this the way news publishing will go in the future? John Sterne thinks so.

"Look at the American model. There, the whole thrust is towards developing electronic versions of mass circulation publications. Many of them are already online, and can be found on the Internet. Soon all newspapers will be available on it."

John Sterne's computer is not just his method of reaching his subscribers. It is also a valuable database

John Sterne. Photograph: Courtesy of Technology Ireland magazine.

and research tool. Linked to the Internet, he can find information on a range of subjects. As an example, he linked into the "A.T. & T. News Online" service, getting into their head office computer, and looking up a list of their latest press releases. There, he was able to get the up-to-date news on the company, at the press of a button, removing a phone call to a press officer, and a request for a fax of the press release as is the more conventional way.

"PR companies are being taken out of the loop by this technology," he said. "It is much more direct and faster, and it's cheaper."

Even when he's not based in his home office, John can produce his magazine electronically, through his Powerbook laptop computer, and send it down the line from anywhere in the world.

John's company, Newsmail, has no "office" as such; his reporter and sales staff work on their own, keeping in touch by computer. He has no headquarters - there's no need to.

This could be the type of journalistic workplace of the future - a portable computer with fax and modem attached, a mobile phone and an address on the Internet. Welcome to the future.

12 OPENING THE FILES

Information and the Law

INTRODUCTION

"News is something which someone somewhere wants suppressed; everything else is advertising."

The central job of any journalist is to communicate information to the public, whether that is through newspaper, radio or television.

Finding that information and getting it across in a clear and understandable way, is the nuts and bolts of journalism.

Making sure that the information is accurate, and within legal boundaries, is also a central responsibility of the journalist.

This chapter looks at these two issues: the source of information, and how to find out more, and secondly, the legal obligations of journalists to operate within the boundaries of the laws covering libel, privacy and slander.

SOURCES OF INFORMATION FOR JOURNALISTS

Journalists need to know where to find information, whether official or unofficial. Their "sources" are developed from the start, gathered and kept for the day when a story breaks and the inside information is required.

And while the campaign for freedom of information has received fresh impetus in recent times, the nuts and bolts of information-gathering remain as difficult as ever.

To write any story, feature or research a programme, journalists look for information from a number of sources.

OFFICIAL SOURCES

Government Reports

There is a lot of information kept in official reports from governments and organisations, often gathering dust on library shelves and in Government offices. Public reports can be found in libraries and purchased from the Government Publications Office in Dublin. Information offices in Government departments can be helpful in giving details of published reports.

The EC offices in Dublin's Molesworth Street also have an information office, containing a considerable amount of EC-related information.

Libraries

Your local library is a valuable resource for information, and librarians themselves can often point to the right direction for seeking official and local information.

The Business and Technology Library in Dublin's ILAC centre contains a huge file of companies and business information, newspapers and magazines, as well as books and reference material with a business slant.

Unofficial Sources

Journalists build up contacts in a number of areas as their experience broadens. Often these are considerably valuable sources of unofficial information - background information on stories, behind-the-scenes goings on in organisations, and insider knowledge of political events.

The Contacts Book

All journalists build up a "contacts book" - usually a well-thumbed indexed and alphabetical book of names and numbers of people worth contacting; direct lines and home telephone numbers for press officers, politicians, senior and well-placed contacts in a range of areas. The contacts book is one of the most treasured possessions of a journalist.

Everything from the home number of the Taoiseach's press officer, to the name of the retired lighthouse keeper in Cork can be found in this book. Journalists write every telephone number in this book, and every subject under the sun can be found in it.

The Telephone Directory

One of the most useful tools for a journalist, sometimes so obvious it gets ignored. Along with the Golden Pages, a good source for names of companies specialising on one area, for example. Thom's Directory is useful for finding local addresses.

Other Publications

There are a number of other publications, containing considerable amounts of reference material. One of the best of these is the IPA Diary, which contains lists of personnel in Government departments, politicians, civil administration, large companies and media related organisations.

Internal publications of organisations often contain names of senior personnel and background information on their companies. Banks, trade unions and semi-state organisations often publish their own directories.

The Catholic Directory, for example, gives the names and addresses of priests in all the parishes around the country, as well as their bishops and superiors.

Reference Texts

These are the standard reference texts that can give these significant background information on most current affairs subjects; most are available in public and newspaper libraries.

They include the Encyclopedia Brittanica, and Chambers Encyclopedia; the Guinness Book of Records; Keesing's Contemporary Archives (see section on RTE Library); Who's Who (particularly useful for addresses or phone numbers, and obituaries), and related Who's Who in Ireland, in the theatre, and International Who's Who; and The Times Atlas.

OBSTACLES TO GETTING INFORMATION

In an ideal world, journalists would have access to all information, and governments and powerful people would have nothing to hide.

But in the real world, journalists often spend a considerable amount of time finding out things that interested parties don't want printed, and the culture of secrecy surrounding the Civil Service, illustrated by the Official Secrets Act, penalises public servants from giving any kind of information to the public.

The culture of hiding information is also widespread in the business community, where accounting procedures and official attitudes prevail against an open attitude to information for the public.

Financial information is a closely-guarded secret; business deals, even those involving the public, are difficult to disclose. When he was head of the Business and Finance department of *The Irish Times*, journalist Don Buckley said information about Irish companies "often seem to be guarded like State secrets of the Cold War era". Legal requirements about disclosure of company information are not wide-ranging.

Local government decisions are not publicly available; minutes of meetings rarely give much detail away. Journalists covering many areas from the environment, to local government and politics, rely on unofficial sources, building up contacts, and relying on insider knowledge to find out what in many cases the public should be freely available to ask.

THE RTE LIBRARY

An Invaluable Resource for Journalists

The RTE library is on the first floor of one of the newer buildings in the RTE Complex in Montrose. Suitably, it's between the TV and the Radio buildings; reporters and programme makers can quickly access this central resource.

"No, I don't think journalists in general are good at using libraries," says its director, Jane Hall. "It's an invaluable resource, and could be used more. Journalists tend not to be that library-conscious, and many rely on their own personal sources and cuttings. One of our jobs is to make them conscious of what we have here."

She characterises the library's service as "a quick response, with an ability and flexibility to obtain materials at short notice".

Newspapers

There's an index of *The Irish Times* articles on microfilm, covering 1969 to 1986.

On the mainframe computer, there's *The Irish Times* from 1987 to 1993, and since 1994, library staff have been imaging *The Irish Times* cuttings on the Windows PC system, making retrieval simple and fast.

With this system, the newspaper articles can be accessed by computer from around the RTE complex, and printed off in various locations at any time of the day or night.

As well as *The Irish Times*, the library has all the Irish Sunday newspapers on file, and they have been on the imaging system since the beginning of 1995.

On a daily basis, the library gets all the daily Irish, northern and English newspapers, and hard copies are kept for up to a year. For reference, English newspapers can be accessed online through the "UK Profile" computer system, an online computerised text searching system.

Biographical Files

The library has a huge range of biographical files dating back to the late 60s. These are still in filing cabinets and card-indexed; it is planned to scan these onto the optical disk system in the near future. All the major figures in Irish national life have been filed under this system, with information from newspapers, magazines and other publications.

Books

There are over 12,000 books in the library, and these have been indexed on the Windows PC system. New books are ordered every week; choice is determined by what the librarian feels that RTE staff will require.

Magazine

From the popular and widely read current affairs magazines, to the more specialised areas, the library contains dozens of Irish and international magazines. Back issues are kept on file.

Journals

The latest journals on a range of issues of interest to programme makers, journalists and technicians are kept. These have been computerised in the spring of 1995, and readers will be able from then on to access the latest issue promptly.

CD-Roms and Reference

The invaluable Keesing's Archives, the update of current affairs around the world, is now available on CD-rom computer disk. So is *The Economist* magazine, the *Times* and *Sunday Times* newspapers, *Film Index International,* and *Time* magazine, and all can be quickly accessed and retrieved by computer. These can also be regularly updated on disk.

Government Publications

Copies of Government reports are filed; everything from the Stardust report to the Culliton report, to the reports of the Law Reform Commission, and Government Estimates.

All the Dail and Seanad debates are kept, including bound volumes going back to the beginning of the parliaments, and the Acts of the Oireachtas are also kept.

Business Eye

This is the online business information system run by *Business and Finance* magazine.

Radio Drama Scripts

There are indexed in the RTE library. So is the *RTE Guide* magazine, from 1963 to 1973.

Access by other Libraries

The RTE Library does not contain everything that programme makers seek, and therefore it has an arrangement with Trinity College Dublin and Dublin Public Libraries, who give excellent co-operative support in tracing information. Trinity Library, for example, is a national deposit library, meaning it gets a copy of every English and Irish publication.

Pilot Project

Since early 1995, the RTE library has participated in a pilot project with five libraries, including the *Belfast Telegraph* and Dublin Public Libraries, making its news information available online.

Researcher Sheila Ahern uses the resources of the RTE Library.   Photograph: Kate Horgan.

WORKING WITHIN THE BOUNDARIES – JOURNALISTS AND THE LAW

Tension between journalists and the law is as old as both professions. The law draws boundaries in which journalists operate - and journalists try to push those boundaries further all the time.

No training course for journalists is complete without a section on the law and the journalist. A working knowledge of the law on libel, contempt, and privacy is essential if the journalist is not to spend most of his or her time defending actions in the courts – and to the editor!

Broadcasting Law

Broadcast journalists must also be aware of the Broadcasting Authority Acts and the responsibility it places on them. These acts also apply in the independent radio sector.

RTE journalists are supplied with a set of guidelines which the organisation has drawn up in response to these Acts. This booklet covers Section 31 of the Broadcasting Acts which up to 1994 banned interviews with spokespersons for a number of named organisations. Now that the order under this Section has been changed to make it less restrictive and to allow interviews with spokespersons for Sinn Fein, it has become less controversial.

However Section 18 of the Broadcasting Authority Act is relevant in that it specifically prohibits:

"...anything which may reasonably be regarded as being likely to promote, or incite to, crime or as tending to undermine the authority of the State."

Privilege

Privilege is the entitlement to refuse to answer questions seeking information derived from confidential communications.

In the case of journalists, Irish law does not award privilege – in other words, the law does not protect a journalist who refuses to reveal his/her sources to a court of law.

The appearance in court of Susan O'Keeffe, the journalist who broke the story which led to the Beef Tribunal, was one of the most controversial confrontations between a journalist and the law of its kind in recent years. It raised the issue of journalistic privilege and protection of sources and led directly to the commitment by the current (Fine Gael/Labour/Democratic Left) Government to examine these issues.

Privilege is, however, a difficult area. A recent report by the Law Reform Commission recommended against awarding privilege to journalists, while the law in England, which does award limited privilege, is actively criticised by the National Union of Journalists.

The Public Interest vs What The Public is Interested In

The bringing forward of Freedom of Information legislation, due at the end of 1995, has the potential to significantly change the way information is handled by the institutions of state in this country. It also has the potential to give journalists access to information about government decisions, and to information held by semi state organisations, as well as local authorities and health boards, not currently available. Indeed the leaders of the public campaign for Freedom of Information have been journalists.

Freedom of information already operates to a limited extent in this country following an EU directive on the release of environmental information legislation. Thus for instance, Cork County Council is required to give information about emissions from chemical plants in Cork Harbour.

It is interesting to note that in countries which have introduced freedom of Information legislation in the last decade, such as New Zealand, Australia and Canada, the vast majority of requests for information have been from individuals, not from journalists or lobby groups.

Privacy

The debate on Freedom of Information has already raised the question of how journalists use information. Irish newspapers have shown no inclination to mirror the excesses of the British press in the way the private lives of public figures are publicised, but there is occasional criticism of how the media handles stories - and invades privacy.

There is no common-law right to privacy in this country although certain protections do exist such as the law on trespass, the court-defined right to marital privacy and the law relating to breach of confidence.

And of course the citizen has the right to the protection of his or her good name, and reputation.

This right is being increasingly used, as the Irish follow the examples of their neighbours and become more litigious.

Libel, Slander and Defamation

Libel is the legal name for defamatory words generally written about a person - slander is the term applied to defamatory words uttered.

Damian McHugh, author of *Libel Law - A Handbook for Irish Journalists*, writes:

"Perhaps the best definition of what constitutes defamation was provided by the Irish courts in 1971 which defined defamation as the wrongful publication of a false statement about a person, which tends to lower that person in the eyes of right-thinking members of society or tends to hold that person to be shunned or avoided by right-thinking members of society."

One might assume that this means that the truth is a defence against a charge of defamation, but it is not, as many a journalist and publisher will attest to, as they settle yet another action out of court.

The campaign by the National Newspapers of Ireland (NNI)to change the libel laws finally seems to be bearing fruit.

At the time of going to press, Equality and Law Reform Minister, Mervyn Taylor, had undertaken to bring forward legislation to reform the law on libel, by the end of 1995. This follows the publication of a Private Members Bill by the Progressive Democrats - and a long campaign for a change in the law by the newspaper industry.

Minister Taylor has not indicated what changes he will bring forward, but if he was to follow the recommendations of the Law Reform Commission on defamation, some of the following changes might be made to the law:

■ that an apology would not be construed as an admission of liability;

■ that a defence of "reasonable care" would be introduced;

■ that the burden of proof, which currently rests with the author/publisher, would be reversed;

■ that the current position whereby the dead cannot be slandered or defamed, would be reversed;

■ and that distributors and printers would be granted immunity.

These proposals are wide-ranging but would certainly meet with favour in the industry which feels itself under a considerable burden as a result of the current law. Politicians, themselves not adverse to taking actions, might feel differently however.

APPENDIX

NATIONAL PRESS

These are the main national newspapers on sale in Ireland.

Belfast Telegraph
Belfast Telegraph Newspapers Ltd.,
124-144 Royal Avenue, Belfast BT1 1EB.
Tel: 0801 232 321242.
Fax: 0801 232 242287.
Dublin office: 156 Vernon Avenue,
Clontarf, Dublin 3.
Tel. 01 8333 771
Fax 01 8333 771

Cork Examiner
Cork Examiner Publications Ltd.,
PO Box 21, Academy St, Cork.
Tel. 021 272722.
Fax 021 271017.
Dublin office: 96 Lower Baggot St, Dublin 2.
Tel: 01 661 2733
Fax: 01 6612 737

Evening Echo
Cork Examiner Publications Ltd.,
PO Box 21, Academy St, Cork.
Tel: 021 272722.
Fax: 021 275122

Evening Herald
Independent Newspapers (Ireland) Ltd.,
Middle Abbey Street,
Dublin 1.
Tel: 01 873 1666
Fax: 873 1787 / 872 0304

Evening Press
Irish Press Newspapers Ltd.,
Parnell House,
13 - 15 Parnell Square East,
Dublin 1.
Tel: 01 671 3333
Fax: 01 671 3097

Irish Independent
Independent Newspapers (Ireland) Ltd.,
Middle Abbey St,
Dublin 1.
Tel: 01 873 1333 / 873 1666
Fax: 01 873 1787 / 8732 0304

Irish News
113 - 117 Donegall St,
Belfast BT1, 2GE.
Tel: 0801 232 322 226
Fax: 0801 232 231 282

Irish Press
Irish Press Newspapers Ltd.,
Parnell House,
13 - 15 Parnell Square East,
Dublin 1.
Tel: 01 671 3333
Fax: 01 671 3097 / 671 4147

Irish Times
10 - 16 D'Olier Street,
Dublin 2.
Tel: 01 679 2022
Fax: 01 679 3910

The Star
Independent Star Ltd.,
Star House,
Terenure Road North,
Dublin 6W.
Tel: 01 4901 228
Fax: 01 4902 193 / 4907 425

Sunday Business Post
27 30 Merchant's Quay,
Dublin 8.
Tel: 01 679 9777
Fax: 01 679 6496 / 679 6498

Sunday Independent
Independent Newspapers (Ireland) Ltd.,
Middle Abbey Street,
Dublin 1.
Tel: 01 873 1333
Fax: 01 873 1787 / 8723 1666.

Sunday Press
Irish Press Newspapers Ltd.,
Parnell House,
13 - 15 Parnell Square East,
Dublin 1.
Tel: 01 671 3333
Fax: 01 679 7452

Sunday Tribune
15 Lower Baggot Street,
Dublin 2.
Tel: 01 661 5555
Fax: 01 661 5302

Sunday World
Sunday Newspapers Ltd.,
Newspaper House,
Rathfarnham Road,
Dublin 6.
Tel: 01 490 1980
Fax: 01 490 1838

Ulster News Letter
Century Newspapers Ltd.,
46 - 56 Boucher Crescent,
Belfast BT 12 6QY.
Tel: 080232 68 0000
Fax: 080232 664412

BRITISH NEWSPAPERS IN IRELAND

Daily Mirror
51 Wellington Quay,
Dublin 2.
Tel: 01 671 2442
Irish Correspondent: Liam Kelly

Financial Times
20 Upper Merrion Street,
Dublin 2.
Tel: 01 676 2071
Fax: 01 676 2125

The Guardian
7 Ballygihen Avenue,
Sandycove,
Co. Dublin.
Tel: 01 280 1971
Contact: Joe Joyce

The Sun
11 Hume Street,
Dublin 2.
Tel: 01 661 9461
Contact: Paddy Clancy

Sunday Times
20 Upper Merrion Street,
Dublin 2.
Tel: 01 676 5166
Editor: Alan Ruddock.

Evening Press
Irish Press Newspapers Ltd.,
Parnell House,
13 - 15 Parnell Square East,
Dublin 1.
Tel: 01 671 3333

DUBLIN LOCAL PRESS

South West Express
P.O.Box 3430
Tallaght
Dublin 24.
Tel: 01 451 9000
Fax: 01 451 9805
Editor: John Russell
Monthly
Distributed in: Tallaght, Clondalkin, Lucan,
Ballyfermot, Inchicore, Bluebell, Chapelizod.

South News
Unit 5
Woodpark,
Sallynoggin
Co. Dublin.
Tel: 01 284 0266
Fax: 01 284 0860
Editor: Ken Finlay
Fortnightly
Distributed in: Ballinteer, Blackrock,
Booterstown, Dalkey, Deansgrange, Dun
Laoghaire, Dundrum, Foxrock, Glasthule,
Glenageary, Goatstown.

Lifetimes
6 North Frederick Street
Dublin 2.
Tel: 01 872 5511
Fax: 01 872 9104
Editor: Tim O'Brien
Fortnightly
Distributed: Southside

The Local News
Rosehill House
Finglas Road,
Finglas East
Dublin 11.
Tel: 01 836 1666
Fax: 01 836 2104
Editor: Frank Bambrick
Monthly
Santry, Glasnevin, Crumlin, Drimnagh.

Northside People
Orion House
55 Main Street
Rathfarnham
Dublin 14.
Tel: 01 490 8666
Fax: 01 590 8326
Editor: Tony McCullough
Fortnightly
Finglas, Coolock, Glasnevin, Kilmore,
Edenmore, Beaumont Artane, Santry,
Whitehall.

Fingal Independent
First Floor
35 Main Street
Swords
Co. Dublin.
Tel: 01 840 7107
Fax: 01 840 7022
Editor: Paul Murphy
Weekly
North county Dublin.

Tallaght Echo
48 Old Bawn Road
Tallaght
Dublin 24.
Tel: 01 459 8513
Fax: 01 459 8514
Editor: David Kennedy
Weekly
Tallaght, Walkinstown, Clondalkin, Crumlin,
Templeogue

The Forum
2 Church Street
Finglas
Dublin 11.
Tel: 01 8640 286
Fax: 02 864 2037
Editor: Declan Cassidy
Fortnightly
Santry, Glasnevin, Finglas.

NewsWest
Unit B
Laurel Lodge Business Centre
Castleknock
Dublin 15.
Tel: 01 820 3299
Fax: 8202476
Editor: Freda Kelly
Monthly
Lucan, Leixlip, Clonee, Clonsilla

Fitzwilliam Post
112c Lower Baggot Street
Dublin 2
Tel: 01 661 0877
Fax: 676 5559
Editor: Michael Dunne
Fortnightly
Dublin 2 and 4.

PROVINCIAL PRESS

Anglo Celt
Cavan
Tel: 049 31100
Fax: 049 32280
Editor: Johnny O'Hanlon
Weekly
16,880

Clare Champion
Barrack Street
Ennis
Co. Clare
Editor: J.F.O'Dea
Tel: 065 28105
Fax: 065 20374
Weekly
19,773

Connacht Sentinel
15 Market Street
Galway
Tel: 091 67251

Fax: 091 67970
Editor: John Cunningham
Weekly
6,106

Connacht Tribune
15 Market Street
Galway
Tel: 091 67251
Fax: 091 67970
Editor: John Cunningham
27,614

Connaught Telegraph
Castlebar
Co. Mayo.
Tel: 094 21711
Fax: 094 24007
Editor: Tom Courell
Weekly
16,000

Donegal Democrat
Donegal Road
Ballyshannon
Co. Donegal.
Tel: 072 51201
Fax: 072 51945
Editor: John Bromley
Weekly
17,500

Donegal People's Press
Wine Street
Sligo.
Tel: 071 69222
Fax: 071 69040
Letterkenny office:
Tel: 074 21842
Fax: 074 24787
Editor: Seamus McKinney
Weekly
9,217

Drogheda Independent
9 Shop Street
Drogheda
Co. Louth.
Tel: 041 38658
Fax: 041 34271
Editor: Paul Murphy
Weekly
13,236.

Dundalk Democrat
3 Earl Street

Dundalk,
Co. Louth.
Tel: 042 34058
Fax: 042 31399
Editor: T.P. Roe
Weekly
16,000.

Dungarvan Leader and Southern Democrat
78 O'Connell Street
Dungarvan
Co. Waterford.
Tel: 058 41203
Fax: 058 41203
Editor: Colm J. Nagle
Weekly
12,800.

Dungarvan Observer and Munster Industrial
Advocate
Shandon
Dungarvan
Co. Waterford.
Tel: 058 41205
Fax: 058 41559
Editor: P. Lynch
Weekly
10,500.

The Echo Newspapers Group
Publishers of:
The Echo
The Wexford Echo
The Gorey Echo

The New Ross Echo
Mill Park Road
Enniscorthy
Co. Wexford.
Tel: 054 33231
Fax: 054 33506
Editor-in-Chief: James Gahan
Weekly
21,800 (combined)

Galway Advertiser
2–3 Church Lane
Galway.
Tel: 091 67077
Fax: 091 67079
Editor: Ronnie O'Gorman
Weekly
32,099

The Guardian
Court Street
Enniscorthy
Co. Wexford
Tel: 054 33833
and
Thomas Street
Gorey
Co. Wexford
Tel: 055 21423
Weekly
Part of People Group, Wexford.

The Kerryman/The Corkman
Clash Industrial Estate
Tralee

Co. Kerry.
Tel: 066 21666
Fax: 066 21608
Editor: Bryan Cunningham
Weekly
33,445

Kerry's Eye
22 Ashe Street
Tralee
Co. Kerry.
Tel: 066 23199
Fax: 066 23163
Editor: Padraig Kennelly
17,500

Kilkenny People
34 High Street
Kilkenny
Tel: 056 21015
Fax: 056 21414
Editor: John Kerry Keane
Weekly
19,624

Leinster Express
Dublin Road
Portlaoise
Co. Laois.
Tel: 0502 21666
Fax: 0502 20491

Offaly Express
Bridge Street
Tullamore
Co. Offaly.
Tel: 0506 21744
Fax: 0506 51930
Editor: Teddy Fennelly
Weekly
17,368

Leinster Leader
19 South Main Street
Naas
Co. Kildare
Tel: 045 97302
Fax: 045 97647
Editor: Vicki Weller
Weekly
15,250

Leitrim Observer
St. George's Terrace
Carrick-on-Shannon
Co.Leitrim.
Tel: 078 20025
Fax: 078 20112
Editor: Anthony Hickey
Weekly
11,000

Liffey Champion
51 Main Street
Leixlip
Co. Kildare.

Tel: 01 6245333
Editor: V. Sutton
Fortnightly

Limerick Chronicle
O'Connell Street
Limerick
Tel: 061 315233
Fax: 061 314804
Editor: Brendan Halligan
Weekly
6,912

Limerick Leader
O'Connell Street
Limerick
Tel: 061 315233
Fax: 061 314804
Editor: Brendan Halligan
Four times weekly
Weekend: 28,500
Monday: 7,500
Tuesday: 7,800
Wednesday: 7,200

Longford Leader
Market Square
Longford.
Tel: 043 45241
Fax: 043 41489
Editor: Eugene McGee
Weekly
25,000

Longford News
Dublin Street
Longford
Tel: 043 46342
Fax: 043 41549
Editor: Paul Healy
Weekly
23,840

Mayo News
The Fairgreen
Westport
Co. Mayo.
Tel: 098 25311
Fax: 098 26108
Editor: Sean Staunton
Weekly
12,000

Meath Chronicle
Market Square
Navan
Co. Meath.
Tel: 046 21442
Fax: 046 23565
Editor: James Davis
Weekly
19,635

Meath Topic
Lynn Industrial Estate
Mullingar
Co. Westmeath.
Tel: 044 48868

Fax: 044 43777
Editor: Dick Hogan
Weekly

Midland Tribune
Emmet Street
Birr
Co. Offaly
Tel: 0509 20003
Fax: 0509 20588
Editor: John O'Callaghan
Weekly
16,000

Munster Express
37 The Quay
Waterford
Tel: 051 72141
Fax: 051 73452
Editor: K. J. Walsh
Twice weekly
18,500

Nationalist and Leinster Times
Carlow.
Tel: 0503 31731
Editor: Thomas Mooney
Weekly
17,170.

Nationalist Newspaper
Queen Street
Clonmel
Co. Tipperary

Tel: 052 22211
Fax: 052 25248
Editor: Tom Corr
Weekly
15,663

Nenagh Guardian
13 Summerhill
Nenagh
Co. Tipperary
Tel: 067 31214
Fax: 067 33401
Editor: Gerry Slevin
Weekly
7,788

New Ross Standard
South Street
New Ross
Co. Wexford
Tel: 051 21184
Part of People Group

People Newspapers
1A North Main Street
Wexford
Publishers of:
The Guardian
New Ross Standard
The People
The Wicklow People
Tel: 053 22155

Fax: 053 23801
Editor: Gerard Walsh
35,951
The People
1A North Main Street
Wexford
Tel: 053 22155
Weekly
Part of the People Group Wexford

Roscommon Champion
Abbey Street
Roscommon
Tel: 0903 25051
Fax: 0903 25053
Editor: Paul Healy
Weekly
12,000

Roscommon Herald
Boyle
Co. Roscommon.
Tel: 079 62622
Fax: 079 62926
Editor: Christina McHugh
Weekly
16,550.

Sligo Champion
Wine Street
Sligo.
Tel: 071 69222
Fax: 071-69040
Editor: N. J. Townsend

Weekly
16,390.

Sligo Weekender
Castle Street
Sligo
Tel: 071 42140
Fax: 071 42255
Editor: Brian McHugh
Weekly
12,000

Southern Star
Skibbereen
Cork.
Tel: 028 21200
Fax: 08-21071
1071
Editor: L O'Regan
Weekly
16,151

Tipperary Star
Friar Street
Thurles
Co. Tipperary
Tel: 0504 21122
Fax: 0504 21110
Editor: Michael Dundon
Weekly
10,434

Topic Newspapers Ltd
publishers of

Westmeath Topic
Offaly Topic
Meath Topic
Lynn Industrial Estate
Mullingar
Co. Meath.
Tel: 044 48868
Fax: 044 43777
Editor: Dick Hogan
Weekly

Tuam Herald and Western Advertiser
Dublin Road
Tuam
Co.Galway.
Tel: 093 24183
Fax: 093 24478
Editor: David Burke
Weekly
11,000

Tullamore Tribune
Church Street
Tullamore
Co. Offaly.
Tel: 0506 21152
Fax: 0506 21927.
Editor: G.V.Oakley
Weekly
6,000.

Waterford News and Start
Michael Street

Waterford
Tel: 051 74951
Fax: 051 55281
Editor: Peter Doyle
Weekly
16,000.

Western People
Francis Street
Ballina
Co. Mayo
Tel: 096 21188
Fax: 096 70208
Editor: Terry Reilly
Weekly
28,001

Westmeath Examiner
19 Dominick Street
Mullingar

Co. Westmeath.
Tel: 044 48426
Fax: 044 40640
Editor: N.J. Nally
Weekly
13, 245

Wicklow People
Main Street
Wicklow
Tel: 0404 67198
Fax: 0404 69937
and
Main Street
Arklow
Co. Wicklow
Tel: 0402 32130
Fax: 0402 39309
Weekly
part of the People Group Wexford.

MAGAZINES

Business and Finance
Belenos Publications
50 Fitzwilliam Square
Dublin 2.
Tel: 01 676 4587
Fax: 01 661 9781
Weekly
Editor: Dan White
11,286

Hot Press
13 Trinity Street
Dublin 2.
Tel: 01 679 5097
Fax: 01 679 3552
Fortnightly
Editor: Niall Stokes
19,682

Image
22 Crofton Road
Dun Laoghaire
Co. Dublin.
Tel: 01 280 8415
Managing Editor: Ann Reihill
Monthly

In Dublin
6–7 Camden Place
Dublin 2.
Tel: 01 478 4322
Fax: 01 478 1055
Editor: Michael O'Reilly
Fortnightly
15,750

Irish Farmers Journal
Irish Farm Centre
Bluebell
Dublin 12.
Tel: 01 450 1166
Fax: 01 452 0876
Editor: Matt Dempsey
Weekly
71,218

Phoenix
44 Lr Baggot Street
Dublin 2.
Tel: 01 661 1062
Fax: 01 668 2697

Editor: Paddy Prendiville
Fortnightly
20,077

RTE Guide
Radio Telefis Eireann
Dublin 4.
Tel: 01 208 3111
Fax: 01 208 3085
Editor: Heather Parsons
Weekly
181, 710

U magazine
Smurfit Publications
126 Lr Baggot Street
Dublin 2.
Tel: 01 660 8264
Fax: 01 661 9757
Editor: Maura O'Kiely
Monthly

Woman's Way
Smurfit Publications
126 Lr. Baggot Street
Dublin 2.
Tel: 01 660 8264
Fax:: 661 9757
Editor: Celine Naughton
Weekly
66,500

PRESS AGENCIES

Clancy News Service
97 Beech Grove,
Lucan, Dublin 24.
Tel: 01 628 2189.
Correspondent: Paddy Clancy.

Ireland International News Agency Ltd.,
51 Wellington Quay,
Dublin 2.
Tel: 01 671 2442.
Fax: 01 679 6586.
Correspondents: Tom McPhail, Diarmaid McDermott.
(Clients include ITN, BBC TV London, Sky News, Associated Press, USA Radio Network News, British daily press; Irish News, Downtown Radio, and UTV in Belfast.)

Press Association (Dublin),
41 Silchester Road,
Glenageary, Co. Dublin.
Tel: 01 2800 936.
Fax: 01 2800 936.
Correspondent: Chris Parkin.
Belfast: Queens Buildings,
10 Royal Avenue,
Belfast BT1 1DB.
Tel: 0801 232 25008.
Fax: 0801 232 439 246.

Reuters Ltd., (Dublin)
Kestrel House,
Clanwilliam Place,
Lower Mount Street, Dublin 2.
Tel: 01 660 3377 / 676 9779/ 676 9775.
Fax: 01 676 9783.
Contact: A. Hill, J. O'Sullivan, C. Linnane.

BELFAST BASED PRESS AGENCIES

Press Association (Belfast),
Queen's Buildings,
10 Royal Avenue,
Belfast BT1 1DB.
Tel: 0801 232 245 008.
Fax: 0801 232 439 246.
Correspondent: Derek Henderson.

Ulster News International,
571 Lisburn Road,
Belfast BT9, 7GF.
Tel: 0801 232 662260
Fax: 0801 232 662260.

Ulster Press Agency,
41 Donegall Street,
Belfast BT1, 2FG.
Tel: 0801 232 323 220
Fax: 0801 232 333 522

PHOTO AGENCIES

Inpho Photography,
15a Lower Baggot Street,
Dublin 2.
Tel: 01 676 4604

Lensmen Press, & P R Photo Agency,
Lensmen House,
Essex Street East, Dublin 2.
Tel: 01 677 3447

Photocall Picture Agency
47 South William Street,
Dublin 2.
Tel: 679 7697.

The Slide File
Photo agency,
79 Merrion Square,
Dublin 2.
Tel: 676 6850

Sportsfile Ltd.,
21 Gt Denmark St.,
Dublin 1.
Tel: 878 7517

Press Photographers Association of Ireland
12 Hazelbrook Road,
Terenure, Dublin 6.
Tel: 01 490 5631

PUBLIC RELATIONS CONSULTANCIES

Adsell Public Relations
70 Upper Leeson Street
Dublin 2.
Tel: 01 668 3591
Fax: 01 668 3977

Carr Communications Limited
The Old Railway Station
Taney Road
Dundrum
Dublin 14.
Tel: 01 298 9777
Fax: 01 298 0808

Communicado Public Relations
Clyde Lane
Ballsbridge
Dublin 4.
Tel: 01 660 5333
Fax: 01 660 5309

Dennehy Associates
72 Merrion Square
Dublin 2.
Tel: 01 676 4733
Fax: 01 676 6865

Drury Communications Limited
10 Clyde Road
Dublin 4.
Tel: 01 668 3119
Fax: 01 668 3878

Edelman Public Relations Worldwide
Temple Hall
Temple Road
Blackrock
Co. Dublin
Tel: 01 283 6666
Fax: 01 283 6711

Fleishman-Hillard Saunders
35 Westland Square
Dublin 2.
Tel: 01 671 5909
Fax: 01 671 5920

Gilmore Communications Ltd
27 Sydney Parade Avenue
Ballsbridge
Dublin 4.
Tel: 01 283 0088
Fax: 01 283 0119

Grayling Ltd
33 Lr. Baggot Street
Dublin 2.
Tel: 01 676 4813
Fax: 01 661 2762

Intermedia Ltd.
22 Ely Place
Dublin 2.
Tel: 01 661 4796
Fax: 01 661 4799

McGovern PR and Marketing
The Harcourt Centre
50-53 Harcourt Street
Dublin 2.
Tel: 01 478 5266
Fax: 01 478 5271

McMahon Sheedy Communications
Consultants
1 Grand Canal Street Upper
Dublin 4.
Tel: 01 667 1133
Fax: 01 667 1147

Montague Communications
4 Wellpark Avenue
Dublin 9.
Tel: 01 837 7934
Fax: 01 836 7814

Murray Consultants Limited
35 Upper Mount Street
Dublin 2.
Tel: 01 661 4666
Fax: 01 661 1936

O'Sullivan PR
Hanover House
South Main Street
Cork.
Tel: 021 271 759
Fax: 021 274 890

Park Public Relations
85 Merrion Square
Dublin 2.
Tel: 01 676 5297
Fax: 01 661 0028

Slattery Public Relations
22 Merrion Square
Dublin 2.
Tel: 01 661 4055
Fax: 01 661 4106

Wilson Hartnell Public Relations Limited
14 Leeson Park
Dublin 6.
Tel: 01 496 0244
Fax: 01 497 5163

NATIONAL RADIO

Radio Telefis Eireann,
Donnybrook,
Dublin 4.
Tel: 01 2083111
Fax: 01 208 3080

Raidio na Gaeltachta,
HQ: Casla, Conamara,
Co. na Gaillimh.
Tel: 091 72235
Fax: 091 72256

RTE Belfast
Fanum House,
108 - 110 Great Victoria Street,
Belfast BT2 7BE.
Tel: 0801 232 326441
Fax: 0801 232 332222

RTE Waterford
12 Broad Street,
Waterford.
Tel: 051 73027
Fax: 051 55555

RTE Cork Radio / Cork Local Radio 89FM,
Union Quay, Cork
Tel: 021 277777
Fax: 021 313170

RTE Television Studios, Cork.
Fr Matthew Street, Cork.
Tel: 021 272922
Fax: 021 273829

RTE Castlebar
Chambers House,
Ellison Street,
Castlebar, Co Mayo.

Tel: 094 22077
Fax: 094 24293

RTE Galway
Hynes Building,
19 - 29 St Augustine Street,
Galway.
Tel: 091 63009
Fax: 091 68827

RTE Limerick
Bank House,
106 - 108 O'Connell Street.
Limerick.
Tel 061 40402 / 48728
Fax: 061 310223
RTE Sligo.
Finisklin Industrial Estate,
Sligo.
Tel: 071 62555.
Fax: 071 69356.

RTE Letterkenny.
Port Road,
Letterkenny,
Co. Donegal.
Tel: 074 - 22696

RTE Athlone
The Townhouse Centre,
St Mary's Place,
Athlone, Co. Westmeath.
Tel: 0902 74543 / 78947
Fax: 0902 78946

RTE London.
4 Millbank, Westminster,
London SW1P 3JA.
Tel: 0044 171 2333382 / 2333384
Fax: 0044 171 2333383

RTE Brussels.
Avenue du Diamant 95,
1040 Brussels,
Belgium.
Tel: 00322 735 3349
Fax: 00 322 735 7621
Aertel,
(RTE's teletext service),
Donnybrook,
Dublin 4.
Tel: 01 7642884
Fax: 01 7643094

Independent Radio and Television
Commission (IRTC),
Marine House,
Clanwilliam Place,
Dublin 2.
Tel: 01 676 0966
Fax: 01 676 0948

LOCAL RADIO

Anna LIVIA FM
3 Grafton Street
Dublin 2.
Tel/Fax: 677 8103 / 677 8150
Station Manager: John Furlong
Franchise area: Dublin city and county.
Talk based programmes with emphasis on local and community news and issues. Also specialist music programmes.
News: Network Radio News and own news service.

Atlantic 252
Radio Tara Ltd
Mornington House
Trim
 Meath.
Tel/Fax: 046 36655 / 046 36704
Managing Director: T. Baxter.
Atlantic 252 is a commerical radio broadcasting station operating on the long wave.

CKR FM
Lismard House
Tullow Street
Carlow
and
ACC House
51 South Main Street
Naas,
Co. Kildare.
Tel /Fax: 0503 – 41044 / 0503 41047 / 045 – 79666 / 045 – 97611
Franchise area: Counties Carlow and Kildare
Chief Executive: Michael Moriarty

Adult contemporary music with comprehensive coverage of local news and sport.
News: Network Radio News and CKR Regional News.
Staff Employed: 12 full time, 15 part time.
JNLR reach: 41%. Reach: 36%

Clare FM
The Abbeyfield Centre
Francis Street
Ennis
Co. Clare.
Tel/fax: 065 28888 / 065 29392
Franchise area: County Clare.
Station Manager: John O'Flaherty
55/45 music/talk mix with a strong emphasis on news and current affairs. Music policy is wide ranging to cover most tastes.
News: IRN and own news service.
Staff Employed: 18 full time, 9 part time.
JNLR reach: 49%. Share: 37%.

Classic Hits 98FM
8 Upper Mount Street
Dublin 2.
Tel/Fax: 01 6616981 01 6616536
Franchise area: Dublin city and county.
Chief Executive: Denis O'Brien
Classic Hits music from the 60's, 70's, 80's and today.
News: Own in-house service.
Staff Employed: 52 full time, 34 part time.
JNLR reach: 28%. Share: 19%.

Cork 96FM / County Sound
Broadcasting House
Patrick's Place
Cork.
Tel /Fax: 021 551596 / 021 551500 / 022 42103 /022 42488/023 43103/ 023 44294.
and
Gouldshill
Mallow
Co.Cork.
and
County Sound Studios
Bandon
Co.Cork.
Chief Executive: Colm O'Conaill
Franchise area: Cork city and county.
News and music-based in city. Opt-out in north and west Cork for local programming. Hits and memories music format.
News: Own news service.
Staff employed: 40 full time, 12 part time.
JNLR reach: 52%.Share: 45%.

East Coast Radio
9 Prince of Wales Terrace
Bray
Co. Wicklow.
Tel /Fax: 01 2866103 /01 2866414
Chief Executive: Sean Ashmore (Acting)
Franchise area: Wicklow.
Mix of news, sport, current affairs, local issues and music.
News: Network Radio News and own news service.
Staff Employed: 17 full time, 12 part time.
JNLR reach: 23%. Share: 20%.

FM104
Ballast House,
O'Connell Bridge,
Dublin 2.
Tel /Fax: 01 6797104 / 01 6777111
Chief Executive: Dermot Hanrahan
Franchise area: Dublin city and county.
Adult contemporary music format, with hourly news bulletins.
News: Own newsroom. Provides news to the independent network under the Network Radio News title.
Staff Employed: 36 full time, 8 part time.
JNLR reach: 21%. share: 11%.

Galway Bay FM
Sandy Road,
Galway.
Tel /Fax: 091 770000 /091 752689
Chief Executive: Keith Finnegan
Franchise area: Galway city and county.
Middle of the road, classic hits.
News: IRN and own news service.
Staff employed: 16 full time, 5 part time.
JNLR reach: 42%. share: 27%.

Highland Radio
Pine Hill,
Letterkenny
Co. Donegal.
Tel / Fax: 074 25000 /074 25344.
Chief Executive: Charlie Collins
Franchise areas: County Donegal (north)
Middle of the road, with specialist country and pop.
Local news, sports and current events given full

coverage.

News: own news service.

Staff employed: 14 full time, 30 part time.

JNLR reach: 59%, share: 67%.

Midlands Radio 3
The Mall,
William Street,
Tullamore
Co. Offaly.
Tel /Fax: 0506 51333 /0506 52576
Chief Executive: Joe Yerkes.
Franchise area: Counties Offaly, Laois and Westmeath.
Mix of classic hits music and magazine– type programmes throughout the day. Specialist material at evenings and weekends.
News: Network Radio News and own news service.
Staff employed: 20 full time, 20 part time.
JNLR reach: 25%. share: 17%.

Mid West Radio FM
Abbey Street,
Ballyhaunis,
Co. Mayo.
Tel / Fax: 0907 30553 /0907 30285
Chief Executive: Paul Claffey
Franchise area: County Mayo.
Middle of the road format with a strong emphasis on local and Irish.
News: IRN and own news service.
Staff employed: 20 full time (some shared with sister station North West Radio)
JNLR reach: 51% share: 55%.

North West Radio FM
Market Yard
Sligo
Tel /Fax: 071 60108 /071 60889
Chief Executive: Paul Claffey
Franchise area: Counties Sligo, Leitrim (north) and Donegal (south).
Middle of the road format with a strong emphasis on local and Irish.
News: IRN and own news service
Staff employed: 20 full-time (some shared with sister station Mid West Radio)
JNLR reach: 66%.share: 60%.

Northern Sound Radio
33 Glaslough Street,
Monaghan
and
Archcourt
Townhall Street
Cavan
Tel /Fax: 047 84444 / 047 84447 / 049 61666 /049 61668
Chief Executive: Owen Purcell
Franchise area: Counties Cavan and Monaghan
Strong emphasis on local news, information and current affairs, Irish, country, middle of the road and contemporary music.
News: Network Radio News and own news service.
Staff employed: 35 full time, 22 part time (combined with Shannonside)
JNLR reach: 40%. share: 44% (combined with Shannonside)

Shannonside 104 FM
Minard House,
Sligo Road
Longford
Castle Street
Roscommon.
Tel /Fax: 047 84444 / 047 84447 / 049 61666 /049 61668 /0903 25525
Chief Executive: Owen Purcell
Franchise area: Counties Roscommon, Longford and Leitrim (south)
Strong emphasis on local news, information and current affairs, Irish, country, middle of the road, and contemporary music.
News: Network Radio News and own news service.
Staff employed: 35 full time, 22 part time (combined with Northern Sound)
JNLR reach: 40% Share 44% (combined with Northern Sound)

Radio Kerry
Tralee,
Co. Kerry.
and
95 New Street
Killarney
Co Kerry.
and
Cahirciveen
Co. Kerry.
Tel/Fax: 064 34444 / 064 34422 / 066 72888 / 066 72855 066 72888 / 066 72855
Chief Executive: Dan Collins
Franchise area: County Kerry.

Fifty per cent news, current affairs, features and sports programmes; fifty per cent music.
News: IRN and own news service.
Staff employed: 25 full time, 25 part time.
JNLR reach: 57%. share: 49%.

Radio Kilkenny
56 Hebron Road,
Kilkenny.
Tel/fax: 056 61577 / 056 62777 / 056 63586
Station Manager: John Purcell
Franchise area: County Kilkenny.
Wide range of programming with popular music base. Strong emphasis on local news, current affairs and sport.
News: IRN and own news service.
Staff employed: 9 full time, 3 part time and 30 volunteers.
JNLR reach: 59%. reach: 43%.

Radio Limerick 95 FM
100 O'Connell Street
Limerick.
Tel/fax: 061 319595 / 061 419890
Chief Executive: Gerard Madden
Franchise area: Limerick city and county.
Community based programme format that caters for special as well as general tastes and has a comprehensive news, current affairs and sports element.
News: Own news service.
Staff employed: 46 full time, 12 part time.
JNLR reach: 57%. share: 33%.

Radio LM FM
Boyne Shopping Centre
Drogheda
Co. Louth
Tel/fax: 041 32000 / 041 32957
Chief Executive: Michael Crawley
Franchise area: Counties Louth and Meath.
Local interest programming with an emphasis on quality news, sport and middle of the road music. Programme format combines informative speech with a music mix aimed at the over 25s. Programming encourages and facilitates audience participation in the station.
News: Network Radio News and own news service.
Staff employed: 29 full time, 15 part time.
JNLR reach: 39%. share: 33%.

Raidio Na Life
7 Cearnog Mhuirfean,
Baile Atha Cliath 2.
Tel/fax: (01) 6616333
Station Manager: Fionnuala Mac Aodha
Franchise area: Dublin
Broad range of programmes, including community, news, magazines, special interest music, features and sport.
News: IRN supplemented by own service.
Staff employed: 3 full time, 17 Community Employment Scheme workers.

South East Radio
Custom House Quay
Wexford.
Tel/fax: (053) 45200 / (053) 45295
Chief Executive: Eamon Buttle
Franchise area: County Wexford.

Soft pop, oldies and country music combined with news and information.
News: Network Radio News combined with own service.
Staff Employed: 22 full time, 10 part time.
JNLR reach: 49%. share: 45%.

Tipperary Mid West Radio
St Michaels Street
Halla na Feile
Cashel
Co. Tipperary.
Tel/fax: 062 52555 / 062 52671 / 062 62022
Executive Chairman: Sean Kelly.
Franchise area: County Tipperary (south west)
Combination of music, current affairs, local interest and community programmes.
News: IRN and own service
Staff employed: 5 full time, 2 part time and volunteers.
JNLR reach: 47%. reach: 34%.

TIPP FM
Whitbridge House,
Old Waterford Road
Clonmel
Co.Tipperary.
Tel/fax: 052 25299 / 052 25447
Chief Executive: John O'Connell
Franchise area: Transmits county Tipperary (excluding south-west)
Adult contemporary music and current affairs.
News: Network Radio News and own news service
Staff employed: 20 full time, 10 part time.
JNLR reach: 44%. share: 27%.

WLR FM
The Radio Centre
George's Street
Waterford.
Tel/fax: 051 72248 / 051 77592 / 051 77420
Chief Executive: Des Whelan

Franchise area: Waterford city and county.
Mix of news, sport, current affairs, local issues and music.
News: IRN and own news service.
Staff employed: 22 full time, 18 part time.
JNLR reach: 52%. share: 45%.

NATIONAL TELEVISION

Radio Telefis Eireann
Dublin 4.
Tel: 01 208 3111
Fax: 01 208 3080
RTE Board of Management
Director General: Joe Barry
Deputy Director General: Bob Collins
Director of Television Programmes: Liam Miller
Director of Radio Programming: Kevin Healy
Director of News: Joe Mulholland
Director of Corporate Affairs: Bob Collins
Director of Finance: Gerard O'Brien

Director of Production Facilities and Engineering:
Peter Branagan
Director of Personnel: Christy Killeen
Director of Sales and Marketing: Colm Molloy
Director of Corporate Planning: Dermot O'Sullivan
Director of Technical Development: Colm Curley
Director of Broadcasting Development: Wesley Boyd
Managing Director, Commercial Enterprises Ltd:
Conor Sexton
Director of Legal Affairs: Gerard McLaughlin.

INDEPENDENT TELEVISION PRODUCERS

Corporate Producers – video production for promotional, margeting, public relations, training/education and internal communications.
Ag-tel Communications
Glenageary Office Park
Dun Laoghaire
Co. Dublin
Tel: 01 285 6833
Managing Director: John Cummins

Carr Communications
The Old Railway Station
Taney Road
Dundrum
Co. Dublin
Tel: 01 298 9777
Fax: 01 298 7528
Managing Director: Terry Prone

Coco Televison
IDA Centre
North Wall
Cork
Tel: 021 395 055
Fax: 021 397 345
Managing Director: Paul Duggan

Diverse Image
123 Lower Baggot Street
Dublin 2.
Tel: 01 6612636
Fax: 01 661 9660
Producers: David Youell, Paula Downey

Dreamcasher Productions
First Floor
88-90 Townsend Street
Dublin 2.
Tel: 01 671 9000
Fax: 01 671 9008
Managing Director: Ned O'Hanlon

Emdee Productions
The Stockyard
20 Upper Sheriff Street
Dublin 1
Tel: 01 874 1044
Fax: 01 874 1954
Managing Directors: Larry Masterson, Seamus
O'Neill

Mediawise
7 Lower Fitzwilliam Street

Dublin 2.
Tel: 01 676 8477
Fax: 01 676 8470
Managing Director: Andrew Kelly

Media Channel
1 Westland Square
Dublin 2
Tel: 01 677 9199
Producers: Conor Quinn, John Finnerty

Midas Productions
11a Herbert Lane
Dublin 2.
Tel: 01 661 1384
Fax: 01 676 7825
Managing Director: David Harvey

Pro Media
Federation House
Canal Road
Dublin 6
Tel: 01 496 5177

Pancom
23 Seapoint Avenue
Blackrock
Co. Dublin
Tel: 01 280 8744
Fax: 01 280 8679
Managing Director: Keith Nolan

Radius TV Production
Glenageary Office Park

Dun Laoghaire
Co. Dublin
Tel: 01 285 6511
Fax: 01 285 6831
Managing Director: Bill Hughes

Reel Good Operations
11a Herbert Lane
Dublin 2
Tel: 01 661 9492
Managing Director: David Harvey

Telegael
Spiddal
Co. Galway
Tel: 091 83460

Tyrone Productions
50 City Quay

Dublin 2
Tel 01 671 8811
Fax: 01 671 8501
Managing Director: John McColgan
Videoactive Ltd.
ENG House
Tubbermore Road
Dalkey
Co. Dublin
Tel: 01 285 4555
Fax: 01 285 5942
Managing Director: Derek J. Simpson

Windmill Lane Pictures
4 Windmill Lane
Dublin 2
Tel: 01 671 3444

POST PRODUCTION HOUSES

Anner Productions
50 Upper Mount Street
Dublin 2
Tel: 01 661 2444
Fax: 01 661 2522
Managing Director: Tom Curran

Screen Scene
41 Upper Mount Street
Dublin 2
Tel: 01 661 1501

The Picture Company
Glenageary Office Park
Dun Laoghaire
Co. Dublin
Tel: 01 285 6222

ADDRESSES AND PHONE NUMBERS FOR MEDIA TRAINING COURSES

Ballyfermot Senior College
Ballyfermot
Dublin 10
Tel: 01 626 9421

Colaiste Dhulaigh
City of Dublin VEC
Clonshaugh Road
Dublin 7
Tel: 01 847 4399

DIT Aungier Street, (formerly of College of Commerce, Rathmines)
Dublin Institute of Technology
Aungier Street
Dublin 2
Tel: 01 402 3000
Faculty of Communications Studies

Dublin City University
Glasnevin
Dublin 9
Tel: 01 704 5220

Dun Laoghaire School of Art & Design
Kill Avenue
Dun Laoghaire
Co. Dublin
Tel: 01 280 1138

University College
University Road
Galway
Tel: 091 24411

FURTHER READING

Paper Tigers, Hugh Oram, (Appletree Press, in association with RTE).
The Media Guide, edited by Steve Peak, (Fourth Estate, London).
The Newspapers Handbook, Richard Keeble, (Routledge).
Broadcast Journalism, Andrew Boyd, (Heinemann).
Forty Years of Irish Broadcasting, Maurice Gorham, (The Talbot Press).
Libel Law – a Handbook for Irish Journalists, Damian McHugh, (Round Hall Press).
Local Radio, Barrie Redfern, (Focal Press, London).

CHAPTER REFERENCE